# GATHERINGS
# OF
# IRISH HARPERS

*1780—1840*

DAVID BYERS

# ABOUT THE AUTHOR

David Byers is a composer, musicologist, writer and music producer. After initial studies at Queen's University Belfast, he spent four years as the Manson Scholar in composition at London's Royal Academy of Music. Awarded the Arts Council of Ireland's Macauley Fellowship and a Belgian Government Scholarship in 1972, he studied with Henri Pousseur at the Liège Conservatoire. He spent 25 years making a wide variety of music and speech programmes for BBC Radio 3, Radio 4, and Radio Ulster, before being appointed Chief Executive of the Ulster Orchestra for the next eight years, retiring in 2010. His music covers most genres except opera and includes orchestral commissions from RTÉ and the BBC. His editions of other composers range across the baroque, classical and romantic periods to the 20th century world of Ina Boyle. Byers writes many programme notes and also liner notes for CDs.

He was a member of the Arts Council, An Chomhairle Ealaíon in the mid 1980s and was a Coulson Governor of the Royal Irish Academy of Music. He has served on many boards, including Wexford Festival Opera and the National Concert Hall, and also on the juries of international competitions. He continues to write and produce chamber and orchestral recordings, most recently for a CD of Kurt Weill.

*www.byersmusic.com*

# GATHERINGS
# OF
# IRISH HARPERS

*1780—1840*

## DAVID BYERS

THE IRISH PAGES PRESS
2022

*Published for* Harps Alive | An Chruit Bheo | Harps Leevin
*to commemorate the 230th anniversary of the Belfast Harpers' Assembly, 1792.*

*Foilsithe don* Harps Alive | An Chruit Bheo | Harps Leevin
*i gcuimhne ar Thionól na gCruitirí i mBéal Feirste, 1792.*

*Gatherings of Irish Harpers 1780 – 1840*
is first published by The Irish Pages Press/Cló An Mhíl Bhuí
on 5 July 2022.

The Irish Pages Press
129 Ormeau Road
Belfast BT7 1SH
Ireland

*www.irishpages.org*

Typeset in 11.5/16 pt Corundum.
Designed and composed by RV, and printed in Belfast.

Front cover:
The Dalway (now Cloyne) Harp engraved for Bunting's 1809 *Collection*.

A CIP catalogue record for this book
is available from The British Library.

ISBN: 978-1-8382018-8-3

This book has been generously supported by Belfast City Council and
the Department of Tourism, Culture, Arts, Gaeltacht, Sport, and Media.

# CONTENTS

*Written for the Harps Alive | An Chruit Bheo | Harps Leevin Festival,*
*marking the 230th anniversary of*
*Belfast's celebrated 1792 Meeting of the Harpers.*

# A HARP PRELUDE

It's all very topical. Or is it? A conservation group in Belfast is hoping to save an endangered entity, like the city's iconic Assembly Rooms. And the backdrop is an ever-changing social and political environment – not to mention parades, marches and rallies.

Nor has much changed over the years. This, however, is the story of the Irish harp amongst all the political machinations at the end of the eighteenth century and the start of the nineteenth. It's mainly set in Belfast, but the story takes in Cushendall in the Glens of Antrim, Granard in Co. Longford, Copenhagen in Denmark, the island of St Croix in the then Danish West Indies, and Calcutta in the East Indies.

Known in ancient times across Europe, Africa, the Far East and the Americas, the harp and its connection with Ireland certainly goes back at least to the Middle Ages. Then the saving grace of the barbarous Irish was said by Gerald of Wales to be their music and, in particular, he mentions the brass-strung harp:[1]

> Chapter XI: Of the incomparable skill of the Irish in playing upon musical instruments.
>
> ... Ireland only uses and delights in two instruments, the harp and the tabor. ... The Irish also used strings of brass instead of leather.

Belfast was not particularly known for the frequency of concerts across the 18th century. Less so for Irish harp performances until the famous 1792 meeting of the Harpers. But then harpers would not normally frequent the towns. By this time, harpers, mostly blind from smallpox or accidents in youth, were itinerant musicians, travelling with their guides or attendants around the big houses, the homes of the displaced Irish aristocracy or the Anglo-Irish gentry. There, they would be warmly welcomed and stay for many days, or longer, treated as honoured guests.

On Friday 19 November 1762, the *Belfast News-Letter* carried this all too rare notice, suggesting that there had been at least one prior performance to this one:[2]

### For the Benefit of a poor Person,

Dominick, the Harper, returns his hearty thanks to the Gentlemen and Ladies who have been so kind as to favour him with their company, and begs leave to inform them, that he intends to perform at Tim's Coffee House next Monday evening, being the last time of his performance here, at half an hour after six. Price of admission 1s. 1d. as usual.

Nor was it his last performance. In Tuesday's paper, 23 November, he advertised a 7pm performance in Tim's Coffee House that same evening. And he would be back.

Meanwhile, two years later, in Belfast's old Market House in High Street:[3]

(By Desire of several Ladies and Gentlemen of Distinction.)
For the Benefit of Mr. JONES, a Native of Wales,
ON Tuesday the 9th of October, 1764, at the Market-House in Belfast, A CONCERT, in which Mr. Jones will perform on the WELCH [sic] HARP several Pieces in the Taste peculiar to the Genius of his Country, accompanied with other Instruments. – After which will be an elegant BALL – Tickets to be had at the Donegall Arms, at 2s. 8d. Halfpenny each.

Jones the Harp would also be back – in thirty years' time. Meanwhile, Dominick the Harper returned in November 1770 to give a concert in the Assembly Room of Bellamy's Inn (the King's Arms in North Street). He was Dominic Mungan (also Mongan) and his performances were long-remembered.

The *News-Letter*, writing about the 1792 Harpers' meeting, commented that 'No one that remembers the exquisite taste and finger of *Dominic*, will hesitate to confess the capability of the Harp of Ireland, and how worthy it is of preservation'.[4]

Mungan, father of the Bishop of Limerick and later Bishop of Cloyne (Charles Mongan-Warburton) and of a doctor in Co. Monaghan, was particularly noted for his really soft playing and lack of 'janglings' of the strings. Interestingly, his repertoire seems to have incorporated more 'modern' music than 'ancient' or 'traditional': select *adagios* by Handel, Corelli and Geminiani plus sacred music ('as might be expected from the purity of his taste, [he] preferred the hundredth psalm to all others').[5]

Setting aside images of psalms and *Little David, play on your harp*, the harp has long been a powerful symbol of Ireland, used by all sides across the centuries, whether it be William of Orange, the United Irishmen or Home Rule for Ireland. And there were the Volunteers of 1778 with their emblem of a crown atop an Irish harp, providing an important backdrop for this harp story.

When most of the British garrison forces in Ireland were withdrawn to fight in the American Revolutionary War (1775-1783), local militia, known as Volunteers, were organised with patriotic enthusiasm to defend against the threat of a French invasion (France's recognition of the United States resulted in the Anglo-French War of 1778-1783) and possible attacks from American warships (the American *Ranger* had attempted to grapple with *HMS Drake* off Carrickfergus in April 1778).

The Penal Laws seriously affected both Catholics and Dissenters (mainly Presbyterians) to greater and lesser extents for many decades. Some of the restrictions meant exclusion from holding public office, voting, membership of either Parliament (Westminster and Dublin), joining the legal profession and attending Trinity College Dublin. The laws were gradually, though only partially, repealed or relaxed between c.1760 and 1793.

Some of this was thanks to the Volunteers' new-found influence applying pressure on the Government to relax the Penal Laws on Catholics. The first Catholic church in Belfast, St Mary's in Chapel Lane, was funded by the

Presbyterian and Church of Ireland congregations. The Belfast Volunteers provided a guard of honour for the parish priest to say his first Mass on 30 May 1784.

Just one week earlier, Co. Longford's Union Brigade of Volunteers, secretary Michael Dungan, met in Granard and passed a series of resolutions including calls for greater representation for 'the People of Ireland' in Parliament; a one year ban on foreign imports 'of wool, silk or cotton, or any mixture of these' to protect Irish trade 'and prevent the fatal effects of emigration'; and 'Resolved, That the Roman Catholics of this Corps feel themselves deeply impressed with gratitude towards the Ulster and other Protestant Corps, for their having so generously approved of the liberal sentiments displayed towards them on all occasions, by that truly patriotic and Christian character, the Earl of Bristol'. [6]

That was the Fourth Earl of Bristol, Frederick Augustus Hervey (1730-1803), the eccentric and extravagant Lord Bishop of Derry who built a palace at Downhill with its cliff-top Mussenden Temple. In matters personal, this 'buoyant and unbalanced personality' was separated from his wife and had an affair with Wilhelmine Enke, the official mistress of King Frederick William II of Prussia. In church matters he believed in equality for Presbyterians and Catholics; in politics he sought reform in the Irish parliament with the franchise extended to Catholics of property (which would have been of limited value as only 300 to 500 Catholics would have qualified). [7]

Tolerance and reform were in the air. Belfast was guardedly embracing the Enlightenment ideals. The search for reason, liberty and new values would lead all too soon to Revolution, but it also engendered an interest in heritage, language and music. Cultural identity was awakening and becoming infectious in these later decades of the eighteenth century. This was, after all, the century of the Scotsman James Macpherson and his more-or-less fraudulent *Poems of Ossian*.

Icelandic-Danish scholar Grímur Thorkelin (1752-1829), the first person to transcribe the Old English *Beowulf* manuscript, was busy exploring the early worlds of Gaelic literature, collecting manuscripts in Britain and Ireland. However, the Danish connection with Irish culture predates Thorkelin's visit to Dublin in 1789. It also has close connections to the slave trade, to Granard in Co. Longford, and to the Dungan family.

# HARPERS, BALLS AND SUPPERS IN GRANARD

The Belfast Harpers' meeting of 1792 had its origin in three annual harp competitions, each with a Ball and Supper, first held eight years earlier in the town of Granard, Co. Longford, close to the Co. Cavan border.

The *Dublin Evening Post*, Saturday 17 July 1784, page 1, carried this advertisement which was repeated the following Tuesday and Thursday:

### IRISH HARP

A Premium to encourage the national Music of Ireland, on the last day of August, at the Market-house of Granard, in the county of Longford: Five Guineas will be given to the best player of Irish Tunes upon the Irish Harp, Three Guineas, to the Second best, Two to the Third, and one to the Fourth.

Some Ladies and Gentlemen of the county have offered to regulate the performance, and adjudge the prizes. — On the same day next year the Premiums will be advanced to Seven, Five, Three and Two Guineas:— The third year to Ten, Seven, Five and Three Guineas. The Premiums will be paid by Mr. Michael Dungan, of Granard.

July 8, 1784.

Michael Dungan, the disburser of those premiums and also the secretary of the Volunteers in Granard, was most likely the brother of John Dungan (1730-1803) who financed the three Irish harp competitions and Balls.

John, from Granard, was a wealthy merchant living in Copenhagen. In the Danish Census of 1787, he and his wife Mary (née Connell) were living at Strandgade 53. He was then 55 years old and the owner of a sugar refinery. He may also have owned land in St Croix, an island in the Danish West Indies (now the US Virgin Islands) with an important Irish community which managed the sugar industry there, first developed by Nicholas Tuite (1705-1772).[8] An important plantation owner was Christopher McEvoy who owned at least five plantations in 1773 – including Estate Granard and Estate Longford – with 577 slaves. By 1777, McEvoy had returned to Copenhagen and was trading as McEvoy, Selby, Dungan and Thompson,[9] though the house of Selby, Dungan and Thompson wound up its business in 1786. Dungan, clearly a man of considerable means, was also an agent for the Ter Borch Loan to planters in St. Croix.[10]

Before condemning Dungan for his connections with the slave trade, remember that many Belfast merchants imported rum, tobacco and sugar from the West Indies – some even owned estates. In 1786 a group of Belfast merchants led by the wealthy Waddell Cunningham (his estate on the Caribbean island of Dominica was named 'Belfast') proposed to launch a slave-trading business out of Belfast. The venture was forcefully rejected by Belfastians, led by watch-maker and jeweller, Thomas McCabe, who is said to have written in Cunningham's business prospectus: 'May God eternally damn the soul of the man who subscribes the first guinea'.[11]

Henry Joy, owner of the *Belfast News-Letter*, reflected the attitude of most of the Belfast merchants, when some years later he proposed a toast (Belfast dinners had a never-ending succession of toasts in those days!) 'to Mr Wilberforce and a speedy repeal of the infamous traffic in the flesh and bone of man'.

Names, and certain people in particular, are important in this tale of the Irish harp. Henry Joy will feature again, but before returning to Granard and John Dungan, we should meet a harper who will figure throughout much of this story. Arthur O'Neill (c.1734-1816) is especially important, not least for his memoirs which he dictated to Thomas Hughes, a lawyer's clerk who worked for Francis McCracken and was also employed as a secretary to Edward Bunting – another important name, but much more of him later. O'Neill's memoirs are a unique source for identifying many of the itinerant harpers in

Ireland in the last half of the 18th century. Checkout the initial draft of the manuscript memoirs online by searching 'QUB MS 4/46'. [12]

O'Neill's memories of the Granard meetings are important because newspaper reports are few and far between.

He recalled that John (O'Neill called him 'James') Dungan had heard that some gentlemen in Scotland funded awards or 'premiums' for the best players of the Highland pipes at annual meetings or competitions. Dungan decided 'to retain and support the original instrument of his own country', the harp, by sending sufficient funds to friends in Granard for three annual gatherings of harpers alongside public balls and suppers.

O'Neill quoted from a letter Dungan sent to his Granard friends:

> … it's to be lamented that persons placed in high situations, and who have it in their power to do the most good by their rank or wealth for their own country, are, I am sorry to hear, the least disposed to do it, I will not attempt to say whether by habit or inclination. I am informed they know nothing of Irish Musick or Irish Misery [= Minstrelsy?] only by the name, so great are their desires to support and promote modern English Musick, and I consider my native land half a century behind Scotland in encouraging and rewarding the best performers on the Bagpipe, which if preferred to the wired harp, strongly evinces our taste — the Welsh Harp is increasing — the Scotch Bagpipes are encreasing, but poor Erin's Harp is decreasing; if I was among you it should not be the case — farewell my friends and hope you will, amongst yourselves, support what I make bold to dictate to you.
>
> P.S: Why not make or establish a fund for the above purpose. I don't want you to imitate the Scotch, but the ancient Irish; Adieu.
>
> Copenhagan [sic]   March 178[4]

Ignoring the obvious resonances with philanthropic arts funding today, back in 1784, Dungan's letter did the trick. The first two Balls successfully took place in Granard's Market House without their host in attendance. Only six men and one woman took part in 1784: O'Neill lists Charles Fanning, Arthur

O'Neill, Patrick Carr, Patrick Maguire, Hugh Higgins, Charley Berreen [Charles Byrne] and Rose Mooney. The same three harpers were awarded the same three places each year. O'Neill again: 'Charles Fanning got the first premium 10 Guineas for the *Coolin*. I got the second for the *Green Woods of Truagh* and *Mrs Crofton*, 8 Guineas, and Rose Mooney got the third for *Planxty Burke*, 5 Guineas.'

O'Neill reckoned that 500 attended the Ball that year and that he'd lost out on the first premium because he'd been wearing his best 'dudds'. Because Fanning was carelessly dressed, O'Neill thought the judges reckoned Fanning needed the money more than him. One of the stewards, Mr Burroughs, 'a tolerable judge of musick, ... was so angry at the decision of the premiums, that he thrust his cane thro' one of the windows'.

Interestingly, if accurate, the premiums were much better than those that had been advertised, though O'Neill seems to have forgotten the fourth premium. Memories cannot be relied on. Indeed, for the following year, he claimed the premiums were reduced to 8, 6 and 4 guineas – again, no mention of a fourth premium.

That second Ball (1785) gained two additional harpers, Ned McDermott Rowe and Kate Martin, but Hugh Higgins 'got somehow huffed and retired without playing a single tune.' Worse, 'a Major Smith who knew nothing of musick was appointed one of the judges, [and] declared, "By God, they made me a judge, because they knew, I knew, nothing about it."'

And those premiums? This from the *Dublin Evening Post*, Saturday 18 June 1785, p.3:[13]

## IRISH HARP

To encourage the national Music of Ireland, the following Prizes will be given at Granard, on Monday the 1st of August, 1785, to Performers on the Irish Harp, under the decision of Judges to be appointed by the Company then present.

Seven Guineas to the best Performer.

Five to the second.

Three to the third.

Two to the fourth.

Mr. A. BURROUGHS,   }

Mr. CONNELL,          }     Stewards.

Mr. EDGEWORTH,      }

After the Music, there will be a Ball and Supper.

Gentlemen's Tickets 11s. 4½d. — Ladies Tickets 5s. 5d.

Newspaper reports – especially when likely submitted by the Ball organisers themselves – seem more accurate, if not for the individuals' names. The assumption must be that John Dungan's friends had risen to his challenge and subsequently added more money to the pot. The *Belfast News-Letter* on Friday, 19 August 1785, p.2, and the *Volunteers Journal or Irish Herald*, same day, p.3, both carried the same report as the previous day's *Dublin Evening Post*, p.3, which referred to the 'so numerous and fair an audience assembled from several neighbouring counties'. It continued:

There were six candidates for the four prizes: the highest, which was ten guineas, was won by Charles Fannon [= Fanning]; the second, seven guineas, by Arthur O'Brien [= O'Neill]; the third, five guineas, by a female performer, Rose Mooney; and the fourth, two guineas, by Patrick Carr. — The decision of the judges gave universal satisfaction, and the evening was concluded by an elegant ball and supper: the lower part of the market house was fitted up in the style of a bower, with much taste and convenience; and the unremitting attention of the stewards, Mr. Burroughs and Mr. Connell, were repaid by the satisfaction which appeared in every countenance. This is the second year that these prizes have been distributed: they are to be continued and increased next year, when it is expected that their liberal founder will enjoy in person the success of the encouragement which he has given to the [music] of his native country.

Mr Burroughs had presumably paid his dues for breaking a window the previous year. Mr Connell was likely the father of John Dungan's wife Mary, and Mr Edgeworth was Richard Edgeworth of Edgeworthstown, Co. Longford, father of the famous novelist Maria Edgeworth and 21 other children by his four wives. O'Neill mentions that 'Always on my return from Granard Balls, I stopped at Counsellor Edgeworth's of Edgeworthstown where I was always well entertained. I taught 2 young ladies Miss Farrell and Miss Plunkett who lived in that neighbourhood to play on the Harp. Miss Farrell play'd handsomely, Miss Plunkett middling.'

Was it a memory of the second Granard Ball that encouraged these *bon mots* in Dublin's *Freeman's Journal* in April 1786?

The Irish Harp has not been so completely in tune for some centuries, as at the present period. Freedom, peace, plenty, commerce, industry, arts and manufactures seem on the point of being perfectly united in harmony. They are seven blessings, without which no nation can prosper, and with which any kingdom must become great. [14]

For the third and final Granard Ball in 1786, O'Neill lists ten harpers (but only nine in the fair copy, though he does add: 'and a few more that I can't recollect'). Two names are new: Lawrence Keane and James Duncan. The others were Fanning, O'Neill, Higgins, Berreen, McDermot Rowe [= McDermott Roe], Carr (omitted in the fair copy), Rose Mooney and Kate Martin.

It was a mixture of triumph and disappointment. O'Neill writes, 'Fanning, deservedly, always got the first [premium], I got the second and poor Rose

Mooney, as usual, got the third', again with no remembrance of the fourth premium! A certain Miles Keane was unhappy about those premiums – 'the most nefarious decision he ever witnessed'. Any relation to Lawrence?

The attendance was the best ever, with 'at least 1,000 people at the Ball'. Accommodation in the town was full to overflowing. The place was like a horse fair with stabling well nigh impossible to find. Lord and Lady Longford attended and, for the first time, John Dungan travelled from Copenhagen to witness it all.

Alas, the Ball was nearly ruined by Bernard Reilly of Ballymorris who disliked Dungan and 'took every pains to destroy the harmony of the Ball'. Dungan himself was so disgusted by the 'indecorous manners of the stewards and others who superintended the management' of the harpers' performance that he stayed away and only attended the supper. O'Neill added: 'There was a very handsome ode composed for Mr Dungan on his arrival at Granard, but thro' jealousy or some other motives he never saw either the ode or the composer.'

O'Neill made a happy contribution by suggesting a subscription for all the 'formerly neglected' non-prize-winning harpers. It was successful, maybe too much so: 'on distributing the collection their proportions exceeded our premiums'.

Despite the immediate success of the Granard Balls, there were no more. Dungan had used his wealth as an example to others, but his best endeavours hadn't delivered his aims. Remember his starting point: '... poor Erin's Harp is decreasing; if I was among you it should not be the case'. Regrettably, there had been no sign of a significant increase in the numbers and the same harpers had been awarded the premiums each year.

As a Granard postscript, and reflecting those times, John Dungan of Copenhagen is listed in the Catholic Qualification Rolls, 20 April 1796, meaning he took an oath of allegiance to the King, the only way for a Catholic to benefit from a relaxation of the Penal Laws and obtain many of the basic rights denied to non-members of the Church of Ireland (the established church).

# THE McDONNELLS AND ARTHUR O'NEILL, HARPER

Another recurring name in the Irish harp story – and many other Belfast stories – is Dr James McDonnell (1763-1845). Born in Cushendall, Co. Antrim, he was one of three brothers, born to a Protestant mother, Elizabeth (née Stewart), and Catholic father, Michael. The boys were brought up as Protestants. All three, Randal, James and Alexander were taught to play the harp by Arthur O'Neill who stayed in the family home for two years, 1778-1780.

O'Neill reckoned Randal made 'a tolerable proficiency for his time on the harp'; James 'made some proficiency also, but he then appeared to me to have a partiality for some other study' (hindsight's a great thing – James became the leading doctor in Belfast); the youngest son, Alexander, would also become a doctor, but he 'made the best attempt of the three (in my opinion), his juvenile years being much in his favour, and before I left him he played very handsomely'.

All three brothers remained friends with O'Neill across the years. James, in particular, would play a key role in O'Neill's future as well as being an important mover and shaker in Belfast life. He was a founding member in 1788 of the Belfast Reading Society which became today's Linen Hall Library; he was a friend to the United Irishmen, though he disapproved of any use of physical force; he was one of the founders of the Belfast Academical Institution (later the RBAI, 'Inst'); and a key driver in establishing the Belfast Fever Hospital and Dispensary which would lead to the creation of the Royal Victoria Hospital.

In response to a request from Edward Bunting, then living in Baggot Street, Dublin, for information about Arthur O'Neill, James McDonnell replied to 'My dear Mr. Bunting' on 8 November 1838:[15]

... My father, who had a great fondness for music, selected O'Neill as the most proper person he then knew to teach his children and he liv'd in our house for two years in this capacity; but my father's death, in 1780, put an end to this study, which we found very difficult on account of the teacher being blind – at that period almost all harpers were blind, this profession having been humanely reserved as a provision for the sons of reduced gentlemen who happened to be blind, a calamity then much more common than at present owing to improvements in the treatment of small pox.

During the two years he liv'd in the house, he was treated as a poor gentleman – had a servant – was a man of strong natural sense, pleasing in his manners and had acquired a considerable knowledge of the common topics, so that he acquit himself very well in mixed society when encouraged to converse – he had, according to the custom of these itinerant musicians, travelled several times over all Ireland, and became thereby acquainted with several of the principal families, who were in the habit of entertaining such persons; among these there were some Protestant families, but the harpers frequented mostly the houses of old Irish families, who had lost their titles or were reduced more or less in their estates. These they would visit once in two or three years, and remain from a week to a month in each house, and it was generally a day of rejoicing among the young and the old when one of those itinerants appeared.

As to the character of O'Neill, I found him a perfectly safe companion, a man of veracity and integrity, not at all addicted to boasting or pretending to any thing extraordinary – he never affected to compose or alter any tune but play'd it exactly as he had been taught by his master Hugh O'Neill [as with Arthur this is written 'o Neil'] for whom he expressed always great veneration.

Dr McDonnell ends his letter with '... and if in the course of human events your singular ingenuity, zeal and success in discovering those ancient airs shall be the means of preserving O'Neill's name also from oblivion, it will always gratify me to remember that I was the means of introducing you to each other ...'

# POLITICS – NEW-STRUNG TO THE TUNE OF LIBERTY

Meanwhile, returning to the 1780s, the political background in Ireland was a bubbling cauldron and would remain so for many years to come. The Volunteers had gained concessions on the Penal Laws, on free trade (British laws had restricted Irish trade), and more legislative independence for the Irish Parliament. Their next move was to push for further parliamentary reforms in 1783 when their representatives presented a draft bill to the Irish Parliament. Unfortunately, when doing so, they wore their Volunteer uniforms. Not good. Their militaristic presentation was seen as a threat. The bill was soundly defeated.

From that moment, the Volunteers' influence was on the wane. Despite the ending of the American war and the return to Ireland of the British garrison troops, radical politics and liberal Enlightenment thinking remained very much in the air, reinforced by the ideals of the American, Polish and French Revolutions in turn.

With greater involvement of Catholics in the Volunteers, an inner circle, spearheaded by the Presbyterian Dr William Drennan, began to discuss more radical reforms and equality of opportunity for Dissenters and Catholics alike. As early as 1785, Drennan, in a letter to Rev. William Bruce, was considering 'a society as secret as the Free-masons ... for the complete liberation of the country'. An 'oath of admission would inspire enthusiasm into its members. Patriotism is too general and on that account weak. ...'

Initially, Drennan had been luke-warm about full Catholic emancipation, but felt 'it was a necessary prerequisite for the peace and prosperity both of Ireland and the British Empire, not because the Catholics had proved themselves enlightened.'[16] The Volunteers, however, were no longer a vehicle for reform. Their commander-in-chief, Lord Charlemont, was determined not to give the authorities an excuse to disband them, and so he wouldn't permit resolutions about Catholic emancipation or political reform.

The Fall of the Bastille on 14 July 1789 fomented many heated debates and newspaper columns about its relevance to Ireland. Tensions were further exacerbated by various pamphlets and books, especially by the publication in 1791 of Thomas Paine's *The Rights of Man* (followed by *Part II* the following year) and to a lesser extent by Mary Wollstonecroft's *A Vindication of the Rights of Woman* (1792). Both authors were inspired by events in France and determined to argue against the conservative Irish-born British MP Edmund Burke who strongly opposed the French Revolution.

It had already been too much for Drennan. He wrote to Bruce in 1790:

> ... it is my fixed opinion that no reform in parliament, and consequently no freedom, will ever be attainable by this country, but by a total separation from Britain; I think that this belief is making its way rapidly, but as yet silently, among both Protestants and Catholics, and I think that the four quarters of the kingdom are more unanimous in this opinion than they themselves imagine.
>
> ... I believe a reform must lead rapidly to a separation and a separation to a reform. The Catholics in this country are much more enlightened and less under the trammels of a Priesthood than is imagined – it is improper to keep up religious controversy, when all should make a common cause, and it is said that you take up too much time speaking against Popery – I should imagine this to be improper ... I think the people are seldom, if ever mistaken in their judgements. If the people are violent, it is because violence is necessary, and all the doctrine of all the wise and guarded men in France was not of half the consequence of one practical lesson of the people – in storming the Bastille.[17]

By Spring 1791, Drennan's vision was gradually coming into focus. Resolutions were drafted to be put to the Volunteers on 14 July 1791 as they marched in celebration of the anniversary of the Fall of the Bastille, but agreement proved difficult. Majority approval was not forthcoming; the resolutions for Catholic political rights were watered down by the moderate reformers (including the likes of Waddell Cunningham, Rev. William Bruce, and Henry Joy), much to the disappointment of the radicals.

Perseverance eventually paid off. After Wolfe Tone published his pamphlet, *An Argument on Behalf of the Catholics of Ireland*, in September 1791,[18] the mood changed and a meeting of the Belfast Volunteers' secret committee of radicals the following month, including Tone, Thomas Russell, Thomas McCabe, Samuel Neilson, Samuel McTier and others, agreed considerably strengthened resolutions. As Fergus Whelan has written,

> Thus was the birth of the Society of United Irishmen, and at last Drennan's concept of a secret society of radical reformers had become a reality. Tone and his friends had just created the first political organisation in the history of Ireland which was open alike to Catholic, Protestant and Dissenter. The new society was dedicated to non-sectarian democratic politics, parliamentary reform and civil liberty for all.[19]

This was the politicking which would have an unhappy outcome for many across the length and breadth of Ireland in a few years' time. In October 1791, the United Irishmen chose the Irish Harp as their emblem with the motto, 'It is new strung and shall be heard' – a development of a Volunteer motto from a decade earlier, 'new-strung to the tune of liberty'. Mary Louise O'Donnell writes, 'The image of the harp had the potential to unite symbolically Protestant, Dissenter, and Catholic, but only if it was utilised as part of a chain of imagery that was drawn from both popular and elite cultures. Apart from the image of the gold harp on a green background, which became the flag of the movement, the Irish harp, as a mediating symbol in a chain of images, was a recurring motif in United Irish propaganda'.[20]

On Tuesday 25 October 1791, Wolfe Tone had a two-hour dinner at the home of Samuel McTier, Drennan's brother-in-law. A discussion on the 'Catholic Question' was hot and heavy with Tone, Russell and McTier arguing against the moderates who included Bruce, Waddell Cunningham, Henry Joy and a certain young musician, Edward Bunting, who will appear again shortly.

# HARPERS' MEETING, BELFAST, 1792 – PART 1

For now, the cultural life of the town developed at a pace. Dr James McDonnell, one of the founding members of the new Belfast Reading Society in 1788, would play a leading part in the harp story, along with his harp teacher Arthur O'Neill.

In December 1791 a handbill[21] was circulated in Belfast and then also published with a few minor differences in the *Belfast News-Letter*, Friday 23 December 1791, p.3. This is the handbill version:

> SOME Inhabitants of BELFAST, feeling themselves interested in every thing which relates to the Honor, as well as the Prosperity of their Country; propose to open a Subscription, which they intend to apply in attempting to revive and perpetuate — *The Ancient Music and Poetry of Ireland*. They are solicitous to preserve from oblivion, the few fragments which have been *permitted* to remain as Monuments of the refined Taste and Genius of their Ancestors.
>
> In order to carry this Project into execution, it must appear obvious to those acquainted with the situation of this Country, that it will be necessary to assemble the HARPERS, those descendants of our ancient Bards, who are at present, almost exclusively possessed of all that remains of the *Music*, *Poetry*, and *Oral Traditions* of IRELAND.
>
> It is proposed that the Harpers should be induced to assemble at BELFAST, (suppose on the 1st of *July* next,) by the distribution of such Prizes as may seem adequate to the Subscribers: And that a Person well versed in the Language and Antiquities of this Nation, should attend,

with a skilful Musician to transcribe and arrange the most beautiful and interesting parts of their Knowledge.

An undertaking of this nature will undoubtedly meet the approbation of Men of Refinement and Erudition in every Country: And when it is considered, how intimately the *Spirit* and *Character* of a PEOPLE are connected with their *National Poetry* and *Music*, it is presumed, that the IRISH PATRIOT and POLITICIAN, will not deem it an object unworthy [of] his patronage and protection.

— *Belfast, Dec.* 1791

To be an Irish patriot at this time was not tainted with the sectarian attitudes of the 19th century. A good example was Henry Flood, the Irish politician, who died on 2 December 1791. To quote the *Belfast News-Letter*, he was 'a man of such comprehensive mind and liberal view', he had served in both the Dublin and Westminster parliaments and left money in his will for a professorship of Irish at Trinity College Dublin. He believed that

> most of the ills under which Ireland has groaned for some centuries arose from the mean conceptions which its people entertained of themselves and of their own powers, from an aptitude, grown strong from long habit, to consider their country as necessarily an *appendage* of the British Empire, and themselves as in a state of provincial dependence on the British government. ... To preserve and cultivate the Irish language, and to excite to the study of its antiquities, and of its history, must therefore have an immediate and powerful tendency to give Ireland a distinct character, and to inspire her sons with national pride ... [22]

Alas, Henry Flood's will was contested and, because of his illegitimacy, it was declared illegal.

The new year 1792 was particularly fraught in Belfast, making it all the more surprising that the Harpers' meeting in July ever took place at all.

Belfast, a mainly Presbyterian/Dissenter town, was divided between radicals, the United Irishmen with a more nationalistic outlook, and moderate reformers who, like Henry Joy of the *Belfast News-Letter*, sought a slower gradual change. A second newspaper, the *Northern Star* was launched early in January 1792 to represent the radical outlook.

There were important town meetings in Belfast; political agitation for parliamentary reform on behalf of everyone – Protestants, Dissenters and Catholics; strikes, lockouts and street disturbances as linen, cotton and other workers demanded better pay (the Volunteers had to quell outbreaks of trouble). Towards the end of the year there were worries about rising prices and possible food shortages (particularly of wheat and potatoes). [23]

A major celebration of the French Revolution with a review of the Volunteers was planned for 14 July, coinciding with plans for the Harpers' meeting. Somehow there was space for everyone!

An initial steering committee of Henry Joy, Dr. James McDonnell, Robert Simms, John Scott and Robert Bradshaw (the Secretary and Treasurer) set about organising the Harpers' meeting. They were members of the Belfast Reading Society (shortly to change its name to the Belfast Society for Promoting Knowledge), founded to set up a town library, which would become the Linen Hall Library.

The *Belfast News-Letter* for Tuesday, 17 April, p.3, announced:

## MEETING OF THE HARPERS.

A PROPOSAL for an assemblage of Performers on the Harp, with a view of reviving and perpetuating the ancient Music of Ireland, having been published and distributed in Belfast and the neighbourhood, in December last: — and the project having met with the support and approbation of such a number of Ladies and Gentlemen as must insure success to the undertaking, — a meeting of the subscribers is requested (at the Donegall Arms on Monday next the 23d inst. at 11 o'clock in the forenoon) for the purpose of appointing a Committee to direct the plan, and for spreading the information generally throughout the kingdom.

Things were beginning to move quickly. Just one week later and the newspaper carried, not one, but two, announcements about the meeting: a public notice and an 'editorial' piece which is mostly a transcript of a committee meeting minute from the day before (a handwritten copy is in the Linen Hall Library's Beath manuscripts). It's always useful to have a newspaper editor (viz. Henry Joy) on your board! This was the public notice: [24]

### National Music of Ireland

A respectable body of the inhabitants of Belfast having published a plan for reviving the ancient music of this country, and the project having met with such support and approbation as must ensure success to the undertaking, PERFORMERS ON THE IRISH HARP are requested to assemble in this town on the tenth day of July next, when a considerable sum will be distributed in premiums, in proportion to their respective merits.

It being the intention of the Committee that every performer shall receive *some* premium, it is hoped that no Harper will decline attending on account of his having been unsuccessful on any former occasion.

ROBERT BRADSHAW
Secretary and Treasurer

Belfast,
26th April 1792

The handwritten notes from the meeting provide a fuller picture. The steering committee now appointed a committee of judges, ladies and gentlemen, 'for appreciating the merits of the different performers on the Irish Harp':

| | |
|---|---|
| Rev. Mr. Meade | Hon. Mrs. Meade |
| Rev. Mr. [Patrick] Vance | Hon. Miss De Courcey |
| Mr. Rainey Maxwell | Mrs. McKenzie |
| Mr. Robert Bradshaw | Miss Catharine Clarke |
| Mr. Henry Joy | Miss Grant |
| Dr. James McDonnell | Miss Bristow [pencilled addition] |
| Mr. Tho[mas] Morris Jones | Mrs. John Clarke |
| | Mrs. Kennedy [pencilled addition] |

Then follows a list of important resolutions:

That the premiums to be adjudged (in proportion to the funds rais'd) in the following gradations: 1st premium to 5th premium, with smaller gratuities to others in aid of their expenses. [No amounts were given in the handwritten notes, but after the event the *Northern Star* [25] obliged with a range of 'from ten to two guineas each, according to their different degrees of merit'. In later years, Arthur O'Neill remembered that 'the different premiums were to be kept a profound secret, so much so that one Harper was by no means to let the others know what he received in order to prevent any jealousy amongst them, and to excite emulation amongst them to exert their utmost skill and ability in playing Irish airs &c'.]

That the airs to be performed, previous to the adjudication of the premiums, be confined to the native music of the Country – the Music of Ireland.

In order to revive obsolete airs, it is an instruction to the Judges on this occasion, not to be solely govern'd in their decisions by the degree of execution or taste of the several performers, but, independently of these circumstances, to consider the person entitled to additional claim who shall produce Airs not to be found in any public collection, and at the same time deserving of preference by their intrinsic excellence.

It is recommended to any Harper who is in possession of such scarce compositions to have them reduced to notes.

That the Reverend Mr. Andrew Bryson of Dundalk be requested to assist, as a person vers'd in the language and antiquities of the Nation; And that Mr. W Weare, Mr. Edward Bunting and Mr. John Sharpe be requested to attend as practical musicians.

That notification of the meeting on the 10th July, and an Invitation to the Harpers be publish'd in the two Belfast papers, and in [the] National Journal and in [those] of the Cork, Limerick, Waterford, Kilkenny, Galway, ... [torn page, the rest is missing]

The *National Journal* was the new but very short-lived newspaper of Dublin's United Irishmen. The newspaper version of these minutes[26] added an additional closing sentence: 'It is hoped that gentlemen at a distance will encourage Harpers to attend; and that printers in general will copy this article.' However, two and a half months notice didn't allow much time for the news to spread across Ireland and for harpers to make their way to Belfast.

Obviously, some gentlemen did indeed encourage harpers to attend – as recounted by Arthur O'Neill. His memoirs tell of a bout of severe rheumatism after he'd been thoroughly soaked one very cold evening. The result was the loss of the use of two fingers of his left hand. He soldiered onwards to stay with his friend Captain Somerville of Lough Sheelin Lodge.

> Somerville ... perceiving my misfortune of the fingers, amused me with reading, and on reading the [*Belfast*] *News-Letter* to me, and the advertisement inviting all the Harpers in the Kingdom to come to Belfast to attend to show their patriotism for their love of Ireland, and to bring their instruments with them.
>
> When I left Captain Somerville's I next went to Philip Reilly's of Mullagh, [Co. Cavan], ... At this time I received a letter from Dr James McDonnell of this town (Belfast) and how he discovered where I was, I never could learn, but the subject of the letter was to invite me to Belfast on the 9th of July 1792 to assist with other Harpers, in playing on that national instrument.
>
> In consequence of the rheumatism I felt my own incapacity and expressed it to my friend, Phil O'Reilly, as I had not the use of the two principal fingers of my left hand by which hand the treble on the Irish Harp is generally performed. Mr Reilly would take no excuse and swore vehemently. "That if I did not go freely, he would tie me on a car and have me conducted to assist in performing what was required by the advertisement before mentioned."
>
> ... my having the Rheumatism still, I found myself uncommonly awkward when I came to Belfast to endeavour to show myself worthy of Dr James McDonnell's good opinion of me, and he perceiving my bad

State of health thought it necessary to Electrify me every day previous to the Belfast Ball.

Dr James McDonnell explained to me the nature and purport of this Ball was to show a specimen of patriotism and national ardour to the rest of the Kingdom which was held on the 14th July 1792 …

It's interesting that Belfast's now leading medical practitioner was exploring the use of static electricity in treatments for rheumatism. Like his fellow committee members, he was sympathetic to the United Irishmen's cause, though he and Henry Joy were moderate reformers rather than radicals like Robert Simms. The clash of dates between the Harpers' meeting and the Volunteers' parade must have caused some scheduling difficulties, but surely the regular meeting of the ladies and gentlemen of the Coterie – meeting monthly since 1785 – should have been foreseen!

*Belfast News-Letter*, Tuesday 3 July 1792, p.3 (also *Northern Star*, Saturday, 7 July, p.4):

## THE MEETING OF THE IRISH HARPERS,
### *AT BELFAST,*

IS TO BE HELD in the EXCHANGE-ROOMS, on *Wednesday, Thursday, Friday* and *Saturday* (the 11th, 12th, 13th, and 14th JULY Inst.) — The Entertainment to commence at *One o'Clock* each Forenoon, excepting Saturday, when, on account of the Review, it will be held at *Seven* in the Evening. — It is requested that the Subscribers will immediately pay in their Subscriptions.

Admittance for the four Nights to *Non-Subscribers*, Half-a-Guinea; the Tickets transferable. Tickets for Non-Subscribers to be had at Mr. Joy's, Mr. Magee's, Mr. Bradshaw's, and the [Exchange] Coffee-Room.

Belfast, July 4, 1792.

On Account of the Coterie, the Meeting is unavoidably postponed from Tuesday to Wednesday.

Nor were the Harpers the only show in town competing with the Review and the Coterie. On the same *News-Letter* page was this:

### *Positively for One Night only.*

MADAM [Louise] GAUTHEROT, MESSRS. [John] MAHON and [Joseph] REINAGLE, respectfully inform the Public, that on account of the Coterie party on Tuesday next, they are advised by their Friends to fix their Night for WEDNESDAY the 11th Inst. on which Evening they intend to conduct a Grand Concert of Vocal and Instrumental Music, the Vocal part by MADAM GAUTHEROT; who will also perform a Solo Concerto on the Violin. Mr. Mahon will perform a Solo Piece on the *Voce Claria*, (an Instrument never heard in this country) and Mr. Reinagle will perform a Solo Concerto on the Violoncello. They hope by their united exertions to render this Entertainment worthy the attention and patronage of the Ladies and Gentlemen of Belfast and its Vicinity.

The similar advertisement in the *Northern Star* (7 July, p.4) added important information:

After the Concert will be a BALL. Tickets 3s. 3d. each, to be had of Madam Gautherot, at Mr. Brennan's, High-street; Messrs. Mahoon [sic] and Reinagle, at Mr. Cavert's, on the Quay; and at Mr. Magee's.

The trio of musicians was promoting its own concert and selling tickets from their lodgings. They were *en route* between concerts in Dublin and Edinburgh and, despite the 'positively for one night only', they gave another concert, 'at the request of several ladies and gentlemen', in the Exchange-Rooms on Friday 13th – again with a Ball to finish the evening. Henry Joy in the *News-Letter*, commenting on the Trio's 'admirable performance' on the Wednesday night, described the concert as 'an exhibition in a very different style [from the harpers], and perhaps less directed to the heart'. [27]

A further *News-Letter* advertisement, between those for the Harpers and the Trio, adds feasting to the festivities:

### *Celebration French Revolution.*

The Gentlemen who intend dining at the Donegall-Arms on that Day, are requested to purchase Tickets, or send their Names on or before Thursday the 12th inst. to Messrs. McKain and Sherridan, in order that Dinner may be provided accordingly.

Belfast, 4th July, 1792.

# THE BELFAST REVIEW

What must the visiting harpers have made of Belfast *en fête*? Fergus Whelan notes that 'On the night of 12 July, the various corps from the surrounding towns and districts converged on Belfast. There was a carnival atmosphere as the town's citizens entertained the visiting Volunteers in their homes.'[28]

In preparation for the Review, Belfast's third annual celebration of the Fall of the Bastille, delegates from the different Volunteer companies of Belfast met in the Donegall-Arms on Friday 6 July. They unanimously resolved that 'we will discountenance every attempt at bonfires, illuminations, or any other of those usual demonstrations of joy, on the 14th, which would, in our opinion, tend to lessen that majestic solemnity, with which we mean to celebrate the EMANCIPATION OF TWENTY-FIVE MILLIONS OF OUR FELLOW MEN.'[29]

The General Orders for the Review were very detailed, with the drums 'beating off' at half past seven in the morning and 'A delegate from each Company to meet the Commanding Officer, at seven o'clock, on Friday evening, with an exact return of the numbers of their respective Corps. Each Corps to be provided with 20 rounds of blunt cartridges per man.'[30]

The *Northern Star* for Saturday 14 July 1792, p.3, reported at length on the Belfast Review, and Celebration of the French Revolution. The different corps, formed into three battalions, paraded in High-street and then marched to the Review Ground, a mile away (at the Falls) where they were joined by the Belfast troop of Light Dragoons and reviewed by General John Crawford of Crawford's-Burn. The brigade then returned to town and began the Grand Procession which included flags of the five free nations and their respective mottos – Ireland (*Unite and be free*), America (*The Asylum of Liberty*), France (*The Nation, the Law and the King*), Poland (*We will support it*) and Great-Britain (*Wisdom, Spirit and Liberality to the People*). The flags were carried by boys dressed in the national uniform of Ireland with blue sashes.

The parade included a grand standard described as 'an emblematical painting, eight and a half by six feet square, supported by Volunteers, elevated in a triumphal car, drawn by four horses, caparisoned for the purpose, with drivers dressed for the occasion, in a fanciful and suitable manner'. Another part of the brigade featured a procession of 'citizens in pairs, and people of the neighbourhood, for several miles round, with green ribbons and laurel leaves in their hats'. Plus 'one hundred and eighty of the most respectable inhabitants from the parishes of Carnmoney and Templepatrick'.

The procession 'passed through the principal streets in the town, and proceeded to Linen-Hall-street [present day Donegall Place], where the whole fired three *feu de joy's* [sic] and then entered the White Linen-Hall, where a chair was raised in the centre of the area, round which the Volunteers and principal inhabitants assembled to the amount of probably 5000, at least'. Then followed the speeches, beginning with John Crawford who included an Address to the National Assembly of France.

William Sinclair then proposed an address to the people of Ireland on behalf of 'the Volunteers and other inhabitants of the town and neighbourhood of Belfast'. Then came the very public division between moderates and radicals.

Henry Joy wasn't happy with the clause 'which expresses the propriety of including Irishmen of every religious persuasion in reform; this, he said, embraced the *Catholic question*, and tended to the *immediate* emancipation of that body; an emancipation, for which, he said, they were not yet pre-pared'. After a debate 'of very considerable length' it was put to a vote and 'the amendment was negatived by a very great majority'. Mr Sinclair's address was agreed unanimously. Needless to say, the company retired to dinner at the Donegall-Arms where an elegant entertainment was provided – complete with a lengthy multiplicity of toasts.

William Drennan, a main architect of the Review, was unable to attend because of the demands of his Dublin medical practice, but another Dubliner visiting Belfast to take part in the Review was Wolfe Tone. He wrote in his diary: 'Drums beating, colours flying and all the honors of War.'[31]

He had a busy time in his few days in Belfast, arriving on 10 July in time to don his regimentals, join the Volunteers' exercises and dine with Captain Waddell Cunningham in his tent.

> 'After dinner the whole company [Belfast First Volunteer Company] turn out and dance on the field. Vastly French. March into town in the evening, all with magnaminity and benevolence. Sup with Neilson and the old set. Very much tired after my journey [from Dublin] &c. Bed at one o'clock.'

No wonder he rose the next morning 'with a great head-ache'. No wonder he didn't enjoy the first day of the Harpers!

> 'All go to the Harpers at one. Poor enough, ten performers: seven execrable; three good; one of them, Fanning far the best. No new musical discovery. Believe all the good Irish Airs are already written.'

And he was still tired. Nonetheless he writes about going to the Coterie that evening (did he get the dates mixed up in his diary?).

> 'Bring the Keeper [Whitley Stokes, a member of Dublin's United Irishmen] to the Coterie. ... Women all ugly ...The only pretty woman [sic] of last year gone. Sup at the Coterie. Sup at Neilson's ... Bed late.'

On Friday morning he again rose with a head-ache, not helped by bad weather, worries about the passing of the resolutions the next day ('Afraid for tomorrow every way.') and unsure if James Napper Tandy, his influential colleague from the Dublin United Irishmen would arrive. He did. ('Go to the Donegall Arms and say O! to him'). And then:

> 'The Harpers again. Strum, Strum and be hang'd!'

How much of this is informed music criticism? Remember Tone was a flute player. Some years hence, on-board ship with Dutch Vice-Admiral Jan de Winter, supposedly going to Ireland in the summer of 1797, but delayed by unfavourable winds, Tone wrote, 'Wind foul still. Horrible! horrible! Admiral Dewinter and I endeavour to pass away the time, playing the flute, which he does very well; we have some good duets, and that is some relief.'[32]

That Friday evening in Belfast, music was still on his mind and he went along to Madam Gautherot's concert – sadly leaving no written critique!

# HARPERS' MEETING, BELFAST, 1792 – PART 2, WITH BUNTING

So the Harpers' meeting is now in full swing, the numbers not noticeably increased on the Granard Balls, with ten Irish harpers and one Welsh harper. Was that a reflection of the declining numbers of harpers, or the relatively short notice not allowing sufficient time for harpers to travel from farther afield? Clearly, Wolfe Tone, for whatever reasons, was not overly enamoured. Nor was Samuel Neilson, leading United Irishman and editor of the Society's mouthpiece, the *Northern Star*, 'as potent a symbol of freethinking, independent citizenship as bearing arms'.[33] His commentary begins:

Although these partial representatives of the ancient BARDS and MINSTRELS of Ireland, to the number of ten, did not afford a very high treat to the lovers of modern Music, yet we may venture to affirm, that they gave entertainment to the musical critic, ... It appears that the principal reason for assembling them here, originated in a wish to rescue from total oblivion such NATIVE AIRS as were supposed to be in their possession alone, and which might prove an acquisition to the musical world, and an ornament to the Irish nation: But in this they have not succeeded to any great degree, for they played very few tunes but what were generally known, though not all committed to print; which is a kind of proof that the ancient Music of this country is not suited to the genius and disposition of its present inhabitants; or, that the incursions of neighbouring barbarous nations interrupted its progress and improvement, and finally terminated the usual practice of it, with its utility, when the nation become subdued to a foreign empire. ...

Neilson points out, correctly, that the ancient bard who recited to the harp 'is but very faintly represented by a modern Irish Harper ... the bard was at once Poet, Musician, Historian and Philosopher. The customs of the times rendered his services important, and he was not only considered highly necessary, but ranked in the highest degree; ... but these times are past and the IRISH BARD is no more!'

He is concerned to measure the merits of the music played by the harpers with 'modern' music – Haydn, Mozart and the world of Madam Gautherot.

It is a question, not yet discussed, whether or not the revival of the ancient Music of Ireland, were it even attainable, would be productive of any peculiar advantage, either to the nation or to the musician; especially at this period, when it is superseded, as well by the circumstances of the age, as the great variety of instruments which genius and experience have brought so near to perfection?

That view has long been discredited and we now live in an era when 'historically-informed performance' is highly valued. However, there were valid concerns in 1792 about the different styles of music being played by the harpers. The winner of the top premium was Charles Fanning, who played the popular tune *The Coolin*, 'with modern variations'.

Bunting, however, thought Fanning 'was not the best performer, he succeeded in getting the first prize by playing "The Coolin" ... a piece of music at that time much in request by young practitioners on the piano forte.' The most interesting harper for Bunting was the oldest, Denis Hempson (also O'Hampsey or Donnchadh Ó Hámsaigh), the only performer who played in the old style – with his long crooked nails.

In playing, [Hempson] caught the string between the flesh and the nail;
not like the other harpers of his day, who pulled it by the fleshy part of
the finger alone. He had an admirable method of playing *Staccato* and
*Legato*, in which he could run through rapid divisions in an astonishing
style. His fingers lay over the strings in such a manner, that when he
struck them with one finger, the other was instantly ready to stop the
vibration, so that the Staccato passages were heard in full perfection. [34]

This is a roll call of the participants as provided by Bunting and published
in 1840: [35]

| Harper | Age | Where from | Comment |
| --- | --- | --- | --- |
| Denis Hempson | 97 | Co. Derry | Blind |
| Charles Byrne | 80 | Co. Leitrim | — |
| Daniel Black | 75 | Co. Derry | Blind |
| Arthur O'Neill | 58 | Co. Tyrone | Blind |
| Charles Fanning | 56 | Co. Cavan | — |
| Hugh Higgins | 55 | Co. Mayo | Blind |
| Rose Mooney | 52 | Co. Meath | Blind |
| Patrick Quin | 47 | Co. Armagh | Blind |
| James Duncan | 45 | Co. Down | — |
| William Carr | 15 | Co. Armagh | — |
| ?? Williams | ?? | Wales | Died going home |

However, the ages given above do not all accord with the *Belfast News-
Letter's* 1792 account – not that age is always reliable (perhaps a mixture of
vanity and poor memory?).

Hempson (given as 'Dempsey') is said to be 86, Arthur O'Neill is 55,
'Paddy' Quin is 70. Significant differences. When O'Neill was writing his
memoirs, he refers to himself being 'about 68' and that was probably around
1807 when, as he says, Bunting had suggested he would live in Belfast for the
remainder of his days and teach 12 poor boys, i.e. the harp school established

in 1808. So 55 seems more accurate – and even that may have been a rounded-up approximation, meaning he might have been nearer 53 in 1792.

Samuel Neilson, in the *Northern Star*, wrote,

> The highest premium was adjudged to CHARLES FANNING, (from the county of Cavan) who, from having the advantages of sight, and opportunities of acquiring a knowledge of the taste and fashion of modern music, has arrived at a degree of perfection not easily attained, and which must have given the hearers a very high idea of this kind of music, in producing, alternately, the most lively, plaintive and pathetic sensations. ... [here Neilson lists the names of 41 airs played by the harpers] ... Professional gentlemen are now employed in taking down some of the above airs, and, it is said, they have a pleasing effect when applied to the harpsichord, violin, &c.

Clearly Neilson would prefer his Irish airs in a concert party or chamber music setting!

His reference to the plurality of 'professional gentlemen' is incorrect. Of the four hoped-for names, only young Edward Bunting was present to write down the airs. The Irish-speaking presbyterian minister from Dundalk, Rev. Andrew Bryson[36], was a no-show. As too were the other two musicians: William Ware, the organist of Belfast's Parish Church (St Anne's), and John Sharp, organist of Randalstown Church (parish of Drummaul), a post in the gift of the music-loving Lord O'Neill of Shane's Castle. So, Bunting was on his own.

His father, from Derbyshire in England, had come to work as a manager at the Drumglass Colliery near Dungannon in the mid-1750s. Bunting sen. moved to Armagh around 1760, probably then also marrying Mary Quin. Amongst their children were three boys, all destined to be musicians, Anthony (1765-1851), Edward (1773-1843) and John (1776-1828). Maybe John would have been too young, but Anthony and Edward were most likely choirboys, having lessons from Armagh Cathedral organist Robert Barnes or his successor Dr Langrish Doyle. When father Bunting died around 1782, young Edward moved to Drogheda where his brother Anthony was now the organist.

In 1784, Edward arrived in Belfast as an apprentice to the organist William Ware. When Ware had advertised for an apprentice three years earlier, he had specified someone aged between nine and twelve. A fee was required and 'none need apply who cannot be well recommended, and who has not a taste for the musical profession'. Did Bunting's mother pay the fee or his elder brother?

Interestingly, the London organ builder John Snetzler had provided organs for Armagh (c.1765), Drogheda (1771), Hillsborough (1773) and Belfast (1776).

The 12-year-old[37] lodged with the family of Captain John McCracken in Donegall-street – handy for Bunting at the Parish Church! Sea-faring Capt. John was a successful businessman who co-owned a ship in which he regularly crossed the Atlantic, trading in sugar, cognac brandy, oranges and lemons. His was a liberal-progressive family, keen on social reform and actively supporting the Poor House. Capt. John was married to Ann Joy, sister of Henry and Robert Joy, proprietors of the *Belfast News-Letter*. Robert's son, Henry Joy became the newspaper's editor in 1789 and was the Henry Joy on the Harpers' meeting committee (not to be confused with his cousin, also Henry Joy, son of Robert's brother Henry – he would become Attorney-General and would be a great help to Bunting in later life in Dublin).

Edward Bunting grew up as a member of the McCracken family, known to them affectionately as Atty. Of the McCracken's five sons and two daughters, he was particularly close to Mary Ann, John jun., Francis and probably Henry Joy McCracken who would be executed in 1798.

Within a few years, Edward established a reputation both as an organist and music teacher, deputising for Ware who had an extensive and lucrative business selling keyboard instruments and teaching music in his wife's school in the town. Ware was also a would-be concert promoter and the 16-year-old Bunting made his debut as a soloist in a harpsichord concerto at a Ware concert on Monday 30 November 1789. It was a Grand Concert of Vocal and Instrumental Music in the Exchange Rooms, followed by a Ball. 'The Orchestra will be enlarged, by the addition of the Band of the Right Hon. John O'Neill. Doors to be open at Seven, and on account of the Ball the Concert to begin precisely at Eight o'Clock.'[38]

On Tuesday, 1 December, the *News-Letter* was reporting that 'Mr Ware's receipts did not do much more than defray expenses'. Bunting was back for the 'Second Professional Concert' on Monday 7 December, playing *The Battle of Prague* by František Kotzwara for harpsichord and strings. On the following day, Tuesday, Ware announced the failure of his concert series due to lack of subscriptions.

Nearly four years after Bunting's death, George Petrie (1790-1866), artist, archaeologist, folk song collector and a friend of Bunting's later years, described the attitudes of the teenager or young man-about-town and gave a most unflattering picture of him:[39]

> Or should we wonder that, courted and caressed, flattered and humoured, as he was, he should have paid the usual penalty for such pampering – that his temper should have become pettish, and his habits wayward and idle – doing everything as he liked, with a reckless disregard of what might be thought of it, ... Wayward and pettish he remained through life, and for a long period – at least occasionally – idle, and, we fear, dissipated; for hard-drinking was the habit of the Belfastians in those days.

The extent to which Bunting involved himself in politics is unclear, though the politicking within the McCracken family must surely have been impossible to avoid. Remember that barely a fortnight after the birth of the Society of United Irishmen in October 1791, Bunting was a dinner guest with some of its inner circle – Sam McTier, Tone and Thomas Russell amongst others. In a heated discussion on Catholic emancipation, he sided with the moderates, including Rev. Bruce, Waddell Cunningham and Henry Joy.

Nine months later, with preparations for the Review well under way, the Harpers' meeting began on the Wednesday as Samuel Neilson reported:

> The Harpers were assembled in the Exchange-Rooms and commenced their probationary rehearsals on Wednesday last [at 1pm], and continued to play about two hours each succeeding day till Saturday [at 7pm].[40]

Cometh the hour, cometh the man! Young Bunting noted down at speed what he could of the harpers' airs as they played individually (there's no record of the harpers ever playing in ensemble).

Bunting's rough transcriptions are held in the Special Collections of Queen's University, along with his workings in other notebooks as he reworked or corrected or refined the originals into piano versions, complete with his harmonisations. He was enthused by the work, thus beginning many years devoted to his studies of the harpers and their music.

Unlike the problems in Granard, Arthur O'Neill pronounced the judges 'sufficiently competent to leave no degree of jealousy amongst the harpers respecting the distribution of the premiums'.

Like Granard, the same three harpers took the three top places: first prize (Ten Guineas) to Charles Fanning, second (Eight Guineas) to O'Neill. Yet again, Rose Mooney came third. In his 1840 *Collection*, Bunting recalled that everyone else was awarded Six Guineas.

Bunting also gave a description of the harpers' appearances:[41]

> They were in general clad in a comfortable homely manner, in drab-coloured or grey cloth, of coarse manufacture. A few of them made an attempt at splendour, by wearing silver buttons on their coats, particularly Higgins and O'Neill; the former had his buttons decorated with his initials only, but O'Neill had his initials, surmounted by the crest of the O'Neills, engraved on silver buttons the size of half a crown. Some had horses and guides when travelling through the country; others their attendants only, who carried their harps. They seemed perfectly happy and contented with their lot, and all appeared convinced of the excellence of the genuine *old Irish music*, which they said had existed for centuries, and, from its delightful melody, would continue to exist for centuries to come.

After the meeting had ended, all the harpers were invited to dinner by Dr McDonnell. O'Neill recalled that 'if we were all Peers of the Realm, we could not be treated better, as the assiduity of Doctor and his family to make us happy is more than I can describe. I remained four days with him after the other harpers were gone away, and then set out for home.'

Henry Joy had already penned some thoughts on the meeting after the first day:[42]

> ... we were pleased with the scheme of encouraging a meeting of the Irish Harpers at Belfast, which would have been more fully attended had earlier and more general notice been distributed over the most remote parts of the kingdom.
>
> The number that were present in our Exchange Rooms on Wednesday last, and who are to continue to assemble in the same place for three days longer, were *ten* – a sufficient proof of the declining state of that simple but expressive instrument, and of the propriety of holding out every lure to prevent the original music of this country from being lost. As a principal motive in this undertaking was to revive some of the most ancient airs, now nearly obsolete, their dates and authors perhaps for centuries unknown, pains will be taken to reduce to notes some of this that have been played on this occasion, which might lead to a general publication of the best sets of our tunes.

Bunting was already on the case and determined to find more airs. Some weeks after the Harpers' meeting, O'Neill writes:

> ... on leaving [Mr Stewart's of Acton, Co Armagh], I met Mr Ed. Bunting as I was going toward Newry where he brought me, with whom I spent as agreeable a fortnight as I ever spent in my life. He took some tunes from me, and one evening at his lodgings he played on the piano the tune of 'Speak OYeough' and I sung with him. ... I left Mr Bunting in Newry and went to Dundalk.

The phoneticised 'Speak OYeough' is the tune *Spéic Seóigheach* or 'Joyce's tune', No.3 in Bunting's first *Collection*, marked *Allegretto*, but performed as a slow air by Paddy Moloney and the Chieftains on the 1978 album *Chieftains 8*. My thanks to Simon Chadwick [43] for solving that!

Meanwhile, the sighted Charles Fanning was keeping himself on the right side of his Belfast fans with a short notice in the *Belfast News-Letter*: [44]

> CHARLES FANNING requests the Ladies and Gentlemen of Belfast and its Neighbourhood, *Lovers of Harmony* and friends of *the native Music of their Country*, to accept his grateful thanks for the kind countenance he received during the late Assembly of Irish Harpers in the Metropolis of the North.

# FROM THE HARPERS' MEETING TO BUNTING'S FIRST *COLLECTION*

Both Belfast newspapers published lists of airs played by the harpers (again using strange phoneticised spellings of Irish titles) and Bunting also provided a listing in his 1840 *Collection*. He remembered that the ten Irish harpers had been 'succeeded by a Welsh man [Williams] whose execution was very great; the contrast between the sweet, expressive tones of the Irish instrument, and the bold martial ones of the Welsh, had a pleasing effect, as marking the difference of character between the two nations'.

Having already spent time gathering tunes from O'Neill in Newry, not long after the Belfast meeting, Bunting travelled to Mayo collecting more airs at the invitation of Richard Kirwan (1733-1812), geologist, chemist, enthusiast for Irish music and eventually President of the Royal Irish Academy.

Some time later, Bunting also collected in Co. Tyrone and in Co. Derry, spending time with Denis Hempson in Magilligan, and all the while being encouraged by key supporters like Dr McDonnell and Henry Joy.

The world of the harp had other complexions. Remember Jones the Harp? In September 1794, Robert Jones, 'performer on the Welsh harp, who had the honour of performing for most of the nobility in London and Dublin, is arrived here. He is to be heard of at Mr. McCauley's, near the Market-House.'[45] Five months later, he too was back (perhaps he never went away?). Music and dancing at the Exchange-Rooms was to be 'for the benefit of Robert Jones, Welch [sic] harper'. Tickets were available at the Donegall-Arms at 1s. $7\frac{1}{2}$d.

In 1795, the *Belfast News-Letter* was noting that 'The pedal harp in London seems to be the most fashionable instrument among the elegant circles'. [46] The following year, 'The new patent Pedal Harp, invented by Sebastian Erard, will now be introduced into all the the most fashionable circles, especially as the celebrated Madam Krumpholtz, in her exquisite performances on that instrument, prefers those of his manufacture to all others ...' [47]

The Belfast Society for Promoting Knowledge which had promoted the Harpers' meeting now pursued the idea of a publication. A committee meeting [48] on 7 March 1793 received a report:

> A collection of old Irish music superior to any hitherto published [had been] made at the late meeting of the harpers in Belfast. It was resolved that it be recommended to the society to take said work under the society's patronage and to publish it in London under the name of the society with a prefatory discourse allowing the profits derived therefrom to the person who took down the notes.

Bunting accepted the agreeable terms and in May 1794, McDonnell and Joy sent £50 off to Mr R. Jameson, a printer in London. It was a longer and more protracted process than anyone expected. There was no news by October when Dr White and Robert Simms took over from McDonnell and Joy. They chased Jameson who revealed that he'd sent a proof to Bunting three months earlier.

Duly summoned to the next committee meeting, Bunting produced the proof which he declared unsatisfactory. The committee agreed with him. Thomas Russell, now the Society's librarian wrote in his diary: 'Irish music discussed. I think it may go on if well managed.'

Two days later, on 6 November 1794, after a meeting between Russell, Bunting and McDonnell, the committee agreed to proceed with the venture. But as time went on, there were still many difficulties and delays. After more chasing, Jameson wrote to the committee in September 1795 saying that he was 'extremely mortified the Irish music should have been so long in finishing but that it shall be very soon sent over'.

1796 came, and nearly went, with no sign of the Irish music volume. Until August.

On Monday 8 August 1796, p.3, the *Belfast News-Letter* published a notice from Bunting himself – and repeated it on Friday 12 and Monday 15, both times on the front page:

## THE FIRST VOLUME OF
## MR. BUNTING'S COLLECTION OF THE
## *NATIONAL MUSIC OF IRELAND,*

CONTAINING SIXTY-SIX TUNES, adapted for the HARPSICHORD and PIANO FORTE, elegantly engraved under his own eye in London, with a Preface illustrative of the subject, is now finished — He takes the liberty of informing the Public, that it will be published by *Subscription*, to which he is advised by the most eminent professional men in these kingdoms, in order to prevent plagiarisms on *the first general Collection* that has ever appeared of the National Airs of Ireland, and that has been long eagerly wished for. — It is requested that those who mean to Subscribe may give in their Names immediately, as the Copies struck off are limited to a small Number, and as each Subscriber will receive his Book in the order of his Subscription. — Price Half-a-Guinea, to be paid on receiving the Book.

It is only further necessary to mention, that this Publication has been conducted under the patronage of the *Belfast Society for Promoting Knowledge*; and that the Compiler has devoted four years in rendering the Collection as complete as possible; during which he made a Tour thro' a principal portion of the Kingdom, for the purpose of enlarging his Collection, and of reviving a number of the finest Airs, of which there were no Copies extant, and that were likely to become extinct.

Belfast, 12th August, 1796

*Subscriptions will be received by*

Mr. HIME, Music-seller, College-Green, Dublin.

Mr. JAMES HALY, Bookseller, Cork.

Sylvester O'halloran, Esq. Limerick.

Mr. Anthony Bunting, Organist, Drogheda.

Mess. Buchanan and McCorkell, Printers, Derry.

Mr. John Bunting, Newry.

Mr. Thomas Prentice, Armagh.

Mr. W. Magee, Bookseller, and the Author, Belfast.

Interesting to see his brothers in Drogheda and Newry playing their part. The publication, when it finally appeared, did not include a list of subscribers, so this was an attempt to garner potential sales. And it was premature.

The same advertisement appeared two months later on the front page of the *Dublin Evening Post* on Saturday, 8 October 1796. Still wishful thinking. That same month Henry Joy McCracken was arrested, taken to Newgate Prison and then to Kilmainham Gaol in Dublin, where John McCracken jun., his sisters Mary Ann and Margaret, and Bunting visited him.

It would be a further year, in October 1797, before Bunting registered his *Collection* in Stationers' Hall, [49] though he would refer to it as his 1796 publication to the end of his days.

He'd travelled to London probably in early August 1797, presumably to oversee the final print run. Henry Joy McCracken, his brother William, and Thomas Russell were all now being held in Kilmainham Gaol. Henry received a letter dated 10 August from his sister Mary Ann, [50] like Martha McTier, an inveterate letter writer.

> We have never heard from Bunting since he left home and as [he] promised positively to write frequently, we are beginning to be very uneasy lest some misfortune has happened him and we don't know how to enquire about him, as writing to strangers in London about him would be placing him in such an awkward situation and hurt his feelings very much.

A page later and the post from London must have been delivered:

> I have just received a most agreeable letter from Mr Bunting; the Irish
> Music is complete, all but the Title Page, and he has a prospect of mak-
> ing a great deal of money by them. This will [please him] as much as it
> does us. ... Mrs McCracken gives William entirely into your charge and
> expects you will guard him like the apple of your eye and keep him and
> whatever might injure him at a distance from each other ...

On Friday 10 November 1797,[11] page three of the *Belfast News-Letter*
carried a notice stating that 'Mr. BUNTING begs leave to inform the Public,
that being just returned from London, he has ready for immediate delivery HIS
GENERAL COLLECTION of *THE ANCIENT IRISH MUSIC*, Containing
a variety of admired Airs, never before published; And also, the Compositions
of CONOLAN AND CAROLAN: Collected from the Harpers, &c., in
the different Provinces of Ireland. (Adapted for the Piano Forte.) WITH A
PREFATORY INTRODUCTION.'

The notice continues with instructions to pay subscription money at Mr.
Magee's in Bridge-street, Belfast.

Bunting states that he had compiled the collection 'with indefatigable
industry' and, as it was 'executed in the most elegant style by the best engravers
in London, it is presumed that the patronage of persons of taste need not be
solicited.' He also points out that the price of half a guinea was set at 'so low
a rate, in order' to achieve the widest dissemination.

In his short preface to the volume, Bunting explains the reason for his
*Collection*: 'The rapid decrease of the number of itinerant performers on the
Irish harp, with the consequent decline of that tender and expressive instrument, gave the first idea of assembling the remaining harpers dispersed over the
different provinces of Ireland. A meeting of them was accordingly procured,
at a considerable expense, by the Gentlemen of Belfast ...'

He explains how he was cautioned not to add a single note to the old
melodies and finishes by 'seriously urging gentlemen in the southern parts
of Ireland to follow the example of the Belfast Society by promoting similar
meetings of the harpers in their respective provinces'.

There are no reviews to quote from, but Bunting was proud to learn of one particular endorsement, which he quoted in his editor's preface to the 1809 *Collection*.

> Dr. [William] Crotch, in his course of lectures in Oxford and London, in which he gave examples of the different styles of music, was pleased to say 'that in the first volume of this [Bunting's] work,' amounting to upwards of sixty tunes, 'there are very few indeed which are not extremely fine'. So flattering a compliment from an eminent judge, animates the editor's hopes with regard to the fate of *the entire work*.

Almost immediately, and despite all the hassle of bringing this first volume to press, Bunting continued to collect Irish airs. In a letter[52] dated 28 November 1797, Henry Joy McCracken in Kilmainham Gaol writes to his sister Mary Ann:

> I hope John [jun.] & Bunting will have a pleasant trip to Magilligan. I wish much that I could have been with them.

This was one of the several visits Bunting made to see the old harper Denis Hempson in Co. Londonderry, though he would now have had his second *Collection* in his sights.

The first volume had been a slow, very slow process. Did the books really sell out so quickly? In just a month?

This is Martha McTier, writing on 12 December 1797 to her brother, none other than key founding member of the United Irishmen, Dr William Drennan:[53]

> Have you heard Bunting's Irish music well played – no – for you have not heard him. To me they are sounds might make Pitt melt for the poor Irish. Not a copy is now to be got, but I hear they are very unjustly going to reprint them in Dublin. Miss Clark perhaps can do them justice, and if when she plays the *parting of friends* you should be inspired with words as tender as the tune, you might be immortal ...

'I hear they are very unjustly going to reprint them in Dublin.' Therein lay Bunting's big problem. His volume was immediately pirated by the Dublin firm of Hime, Gough, and W. Power, and the London firm of W. Power & J. Power. As late as c.1820 it was still being pirated – this time by another Dublin firm, I. Willis of 7 Westmorland Street. [54]

In 1802, Isaac Warrin, bookseller and stationer at the Belfast Circulating Library, 20 High-street, was advertising *Bunting's Ancient Music* at 11s. 4½d.

———

It's worth stepping back to consider everything that had happened since the Harpers' meeting. The briefest of brief surveys should mention events in France, with the execution of Louis XVI in January 1793 and the declaration of war on Britain and Ireland by the French revolutionary government, both of which fairly dampened the enthusiasm of many of the Volunteers. In January that year the Dublin Volunteers were suppressed and banned from holding conventions and importing arms. The Belfast Volunteers suffered the same fate in March.

Tension racked up another notch that same year when the government suspended Habeus Corpus (detention without charge) to deter any rebellion arising from the French Revolution. In 1794, the authorities, increasingly worried by revolutionary talk and a potential French invasion, cracked down, suppressing the United Irishmen, who had been building alliances with the Catholic Defenders. In response the United Irishmen reorganised as a secret society, eventually looking to France to help their cause.

The authorities permitted Wolfe Tone to leave the country lest he became a martyr. He arrived in Belfast from Dublin, *en route* to the United States, in May 1795. His couple of weeks in the town included the famous MacArt's Fort meeting on the Cave Hill when, along with Thomas Russell, Henry Joy and others he took a solemn oath, 'never to desist in our efforts until we had subverted the authority of England over our country and declared our independence'.

Before setting sail there was an evening for Belfast friends, including Dr James McDonnell, to say farewell to the Tone family. Bunting played some Irish airs, ending with *The Parting of Friends*. The melody and Bunting's performance were said to have reduced Matilda Tone, Wolfe's wife, to tears.

Increasingly bitter disturbances between the Protestant Peep o' Day Boys and the Catholic Defenders led to the formation of the Orange Order in September 1795, creating subdivisions amongst the Protestants and Dissenters, and weakening the power base of the United Irishmen.

That year, 1795, the *Northern Star* presses issued what was hoped to be the first number of a new Irish language magazine, *Bolg an tSolair* or *Gaelic Magazine*.

The Preface mentions that 'Those who delight in Irish music (which seems greatly to prevail at present) shall also be entertained with the choicest songs and airs'. There is no notated music included, but song texts are provided in both Irish and English, notably the Cavan poet and harper Charles McCabe's *Elegy on the death of Carolan* and Carolan's own *Gracey Nugent* and *Mable Kelly*. The English translations were by Co. Cavan-born Charlotte Brooke (?1750-1793). The music of both songs would be included in Bunting's then forthcoming first *Collection*.

In December 1796 Wolfe Tone was aboard one of the French ships which arrived off Bantry Bay with a large French invasion force. The mission failed, defeated by atrocious weather, and the would-be invaders returned to France with many losses.

William, another McCracken brother, was arrested in a round-up in March 1797 and he was moved to Kilmainham Gaol, joining his brother Henry and Thomas Russell.

The *Northern Star* office had been raided several times, but now the building and its presses were destroyed by a mob of Monaghan militia men in May 1797.

# TWO REBELLIONS
# AND BUNTING AT WORK

The revolutionary turmoil, the invasion scares, the threats of transportation or death, and at the same time living with one of the key radical families, with two of its sons in Kilmainham Gaol, must have contributed to the slippage in Bunting's publication timetable.

The two McCracken brothers were released in December 1797, but Russell remained in gaol for another four years, detained at Fort George in Scotland along with Samuel Neilson and Robert Simms. Russell was a good and close friend to both Bunting and Mary Ann McCracken.

By all accounts, Bunting's first *Collection* of 66 airs had been well received, as verified by the pirated editions, but there was little press comment, probably for obvious Rebellion reasons. Timing is everything – then as now.

Martha McTier, mentioning Bunting 'the famous musician' to Drennan, her brother, early in 1798, suggested 'it would be worth your while to try if you could hear him play his Irish music – sugar plums or sweeties is his greatest temptation for he despises both money and praise and is thought a good-hearted original'. [55]

It probably wasn't the best time to suggest Drennan listen to music. The Rebellion began, as it would continue, haphazardly around Dublin in late May, then Wexford, Antrim, Saintfield and Ballynahinch before a final defeat in mid-July. Thousands died. There were sporadic outbreaks for some time, encouraged by a French force landing in Mayo in August. Another larger French force tried to land in Lough Swilly, Co. Donegal, but was defeated without ever landing. With them was Wolfe Tone who was arrested but evaded his hanging by committing a botched suicide in Dublin.

Henry Joy McCracken commanded the Antrim rebels against the Crown forces but was defeated. He went on the run and Mary Ann met him twice with essential supplies. He was eventually captured, tried, sentenced and hanged on 17 July 1798 in High-street outside the Market House. Afterwards, as she'd promised her brother, Mary Ann wrote to Russell to tell him her brother had done his duty. 'I accompanied him to the scaffold, where I wished to remain till the last, but was not even permitted to have that gratification but was forcibly torn from him by the General's orders (at least so I was told).'[56]

The General (Sir George Nugent), arranged for the body to be cut down promptly and not be decapitated. Mary Ann sent for Dr McDonnell to attempt resuscitation, but, for whatever reason, he wasn't available and sent his surgeon brother Alexander – to no avail.

The Rebellion was effectively at an end. Seeking a properly independent Irish Parliament, it had achieved the opposite. The Irish Parliament had had a measure of legislative independence, though it was exclusively in the hands of the Protestant Ascendancy. Undermined and discredited by the Rebellion, and now helped by old-fashioned corruption and intimidation, the Act of Union 1800 removed the separate Irish Parliament altogether.

The political climate changed considerably, and not necessarily for the better. The radical and reformist zeal of so many Presbyterian Dissenters in the north melted away in the face of increasing sectarian tensions.

The shared interest in Irish music and antiquities by Protestant, Dissenter and Catholic alike, had been part of a liberal patriotic outlook. Barra Boydell[57] points out that 'while nationalist sentiments begin to assert themselves under the United Irishmen, their use of Irish music and of harp symbolism remained within the essentially antiquarian mould of the later eighteenth century'. He quotes Joep Leersen:[58]

In the newly sectarian climate, the optimistic and philanthropic ideals of Patriotism floundered ... The national ideal which survived most effectively into the nineteenth century was not the conciliatory, paternalistic Patriot model but rather the insurrectionary separatist one.

There was one last attempt at insurrection. Robert Emmet and friends set up a new Society of United Irishmen in Dublin and solicited another French invasion. Their plot to attack Dublin Castle in July 1803 was infiltrated and the rising failed to gather the expected support, apart from 'a motley assemblage of armed men, a great number ... under the evident excitement of drink'. Emmet was captured, tried and sentenced to be hung, drawn and quartered in September.

Emmet's Rebellion impinges on the harp story through Thomas Russell who had been released from Fort George, Inverness, in June 1802 to exile in Hamburg. From thence he travelled to Paris to assist Emmet's efforts to raise a French invasion of Ireland. He then returned to the north of Ireland only to find a general disillusionment following the 1798 Rebellion. Russell, now a wanted man with a price of £1,500 on his head, avoided arrest for several weeks.

To the great disgust of many former friends and colleagues, Dr McDonnell gave £50 to the reward and signed a public petition against Russell. In later life he said, 'I had not done it an hour until I wished of all things it was undone.' Many didn't speak to McDonnell for a long time after that. William Drennan, in a poem attached to an undated letter to Martha McTier, dubbed McDonnell 'The Brutus of Belfast' in his *Epitaph on the Living*.[59]

There was another casualty of Russell's trial which had an even greater impact on Bunting and his next volume. His collecting of airs had continued after 1797 encouraged as it was by the Society for Promoting Knowledge and its librarian Thomas Russell.

The McCracken family was also a considerable help in these years, not acknowledged in the eventual 1809 publication, probably to avoid any publicity for their own sake. In 1802 the family helped finance the Irish language scholar Patrick Lynch (Padraig Ó Loinsigh) to collect further airs and many song texts in Irish. Unwillingly, he was 'persuaded' to testify against Russell at his trial on 20 October 1803 in Downpatrick. Russell was executed the next day and Lynch wasn't heard from again. Nor did Bunting include in his work any of the nearly two hundred Irish song texts collected by Lynch. Fortunately, they survive as part of the Bunting Collection at Queen's University, Belfast.

The McCracken family was financially ruined by the expense of Russell's trial. Mary Ann had provided bribery money to effect Russell's escape and then she paid the considerable fees for his defence counsel.

One beneficiary of the rise in nationalism and republicanism in the new Romantic era was Thomas Moore and his music arranger Sir John Stevenson. When the first two volumes of Moore's *A Selection of Irish Melodies* were published in 1808, Bunting was incensed that Moore had used so many of 'his' tunes. Worse, often those tunes had been adapted to fit the words – Stevenson's fault.

Not so, said Moore, writing in his diary in 1840, having just received Bunting's newly published third Collection and dismissing that as 'a mere mess of trash'.

> [Bunting] lays the blame of all these alterations upon Stevenson, but poor Sir John was entirely innocent of them; as the whole task of selecting the airs and in some instances shaping them thus, in particular passages, to the general sentiment, which the melody appeared to me to express was undertaken solely by myself. Had I not ventured on these very admissible liberties many of the songs now most known and popular would have been still sleeping with all their authentic dross about them in Mr Bunting's first Volume. [60]

Bunting's frustration and anger surely comes through in harper Arthur O'Neill's memoirs, dating from not long after Moore's April 1808 first publications.

> [I] will endeavour to show in the conclusion of this poor narrative how folly and fashion will intrude upon the real merits of those who take pains in encouraging the works of a Sir John Plagiarist – or a Sir John Selector – or a Sir John Innovator, or a Sir John Stevenson. If my friend hereafter named, should seek for the empty title of a Knight Bachelor, if a Townsend or a Rutland were to visit this country again he might be sure perhaps [of] being appointed to a similar title of Honour. But this Barren Knight should in my opinion confine himself to his business in Dublin and not interfere with Mr Bunting or his business, and I will

endeavour before I conclude these memoirs to draw (as blind as I am) a contrast between the revivor and restorer of ancient Irish musick and any titled upstart that may endeavour to plaster himself or his works upon those who will not take pains to look for Edward Bunting's works. [61]

That's quite a tirade! 'Townsend' was George Townshend, appointed first Lord Lieutenant of Ireland in 1767. He was succeeded by the 4th Duke of Rutland in 1784. O'Neill, or his transcriber Thomas Hughes, preserves good decorum by notating the culprit as Sir John S—v—n in his fair copy. Likewise, sparing his blushes, the fair copy simply has Mr. B—g and Mr. B.

Bunting toiled sporadically on his second *Collection*, travelling in Roscommon and Cavan in 1800. Patrick Lynch collected songs and texts in Connacht in 1802, initially on his own (there are letters to John McCracken, jun. looking for funds; when these went unanswered, Lynch wrote to Mary Ann, mentioning Westport, and Ballina in Co. Mayo), but eventually he was joined by Bunting. They also visited Castlebar, Ballina and Westport in Co Mayo. On the return to Dublin, Bunting also collected through Tipperary, Laois and Kildare.

'Toiled sporadically', because all the while, Bunting had his music career to think about. In 1801 the First Presbyterian Church received 'a very liberal proposal from Mr. Edward Bunting respecting the purchase of an organ'. [62] His offer was politely turned down; maybe that was the 'elegant new chamber organ', built by Samuel Green, he advertised for sale, along with a Broadwood Grand Piano Forte, in June 1803. [63]

Along with his trade in selling pianos for Broadwood, Bunting was also a concert promoter. He planned a series of eight concerts to be held in the Donegall Arms from 25 July 1800. [64] His artists included a young violinist Master Owens and, from Dublin, the harpist Seybold, who had been featured in the Crow Street Theatre's 1796-97 season as 'Master Seybold' who had accompanied the German soprano Madam Mara and also played 'a grand sonata on the pedal harp'.

Writing in the introductory notes to his 1840 collection, Bunting extolled the Magilligan harper Denis Hempson for his articulation and ornamentation, including his shakes (another word for trills). He then added a footnote:

The late Mr Seybold, the celebrated performer on the Pedal Harp, being in a gentleman's house in Belfast, in 1800, when Arthur O'Neill was present, declared his admiration of the old man's shake on the Irish harp, which was performed apparently with the greatest ease and execution; admitting that he could not do it himself in the same manner on his own instrument, the shake being of the greatest difficulty on every species of harp. [65]

The pedal harp surfaced again in 1802 when Bunting took part in a concert with Mme Dupree, 'élève of Krumpholtz'. She had arrived in Belfast in early September, announcing that

Ladies that wish to take lessons may hear a specimen of her performance from 11 o'clock in the morning till 3, at No.5, Bridge-street, where Sebastian Erard's celebrated Patent Harps are sold, and fine Italian strings. [66]

On Tuesday, 12 October 1802 Mme Dupree gave a 'Grand Concert and Ball at the Exchange Rooms, Belfast, under the patronage of the Marchioness of Donegall'.

Now you're talking – this was indeed a class act! Unlike young ladies with their pedal harp, Bunting, despite being Belfast's 'Mr Music', never enjoyed the patronage of the Donegall family, the town's principal landlords, formerly absentee landlords, but now taking up residence in Donegall Place.

Amongst seven major items, topped and tailed by Haydn and Mozart, there was a sonata for harp, violin and cello by Dussek, a grand duet for harp and piano forte (Mme Dupree and Mr. Bunting), and a harp concerto by Krumpholtz (who had married the lady who taught Dupree (Mme Krumpholtz), who then ran off with the composer Dussek, who in turn ran off with a Scottish singer and harpist Sophia Corri in 1792). Bunting also played a piano concerto by Viotti. [67]

In July 1805, Madam Dussek, Sophia Corri herself, advertised 'that she intends giving a Grand Concert at which she will sing and perform on the harp and piano-forte. After the concert, a ball.' Most unhelpfully she didn't mention where or when![68]

Late in 1805 or early 1806, Bunting successfully convinced Belfast's Second Presbyterian Church that they should have an organ. He persuaded a London-based organ-builder, Stephen White, to come to Belfast where he had his workshop, and probably his home, in Orr's-entry, between High-street and Rosemary-street, parallel with modern day Bridge Street. Orr's-entry was destroyed in the Belfast blitz of 1941 which also destroyed the Third Presbyterian Church in Rosemary Street.

Stephen White's first Belfast-built instrument was for the Rev. Dr. Drummond's Second Presbyterian Church where Edward Bunting, William Ware's former apprentice and deputy organist for St Anne's Parish Church, was appointed its first organist.

> We are happy to inform the public, that the first organ which has been introduced into a Protestant Dissenting Meeting House, in Ulster, will be touched by the masterly hand of Mr. Bunting on Sunday next [7 September 1806].[69]

Some days later:

> On Sunday last, the new Organ ... was opened by Mr. Bunting, with the music of the old 100th psalm, the composition, as Handel said, of Martin Luther, the Reformer. The instrument was conducted with chaste gravity, suited to the simplicity of Presbyterian worship; and the finest effect produced by an admirable finger directed by pure taste.[70]

Another report credited the organ-builder:

> This [the Second Church] is the first Congregation of Protestant Dissenters, in the North of Ireland, which has introduced an organ into the public worship. It will be played by Mr. EDWARD BUNTING, whose musical talents are well known and acknowledged. It has been built by

Mr. WHITE, an ingenious mechanic from London, and is constructed so as to acquire considerable power from the use of pedals. – The organ is reckoned by judges one of the best in this part of the country.[71]

After completing the organ for Bunting's church, White's next large instrument, c.1807, was for Thomas Hull, dancing master and master of ceremonies for Belfast's Subscription Assemblies, the regular society balls in the Assembly Rooms. It was built on a large scale with 'pedal pipes and is constructed to play with barrels as well as the fingers.'[72]

That instrument eventually found a home in the soon-to-be built Chapel of Ease (St George's, High-street, Belfast) between 1817 and 1824. And coincidentally, the new organist in St George's in 1817 was none other than Edward Bunting – though marriage and a new life in Dublin beckoned just two years later.

Bunting's concert promotions at this time included two concerts in Belfast in 1807 (in the Theatre) and another in 1808 (in the Exchange Assembly Room) by the great Italian soprano Angelica Catalani (1780-1849), only 26 years old on her first visit. The concerts were given 'under the direction of Mr. Bunting, who will preside at the Piano-Forte'.

Over the years, Bunting and Catalani met on a number of occasions. Once, she was so delighted with Bunting's performance of some of the Irish airs that she took a diamond ring off her finger and presented the ring to Bunting.[73] Another anecdote, from 1829 during Catalani's last visit to Dublin (she was approaching 50 years of age), was recalled by George Petrie:[74]

Catalani – 'Well, my dear Mr. Bunting, how glad I am to see you looking so strong and well.'

Bunting, with a shrug – 'Ugh, ugh, no madam, I'm growing fat and lazy like an old dog as I am.'

Catalani, looking alarmed and thoughtful – 'Ah, indeed, Mr. Bunting – and I too am growing fat and lazy, like an old dog as I am – no, that's not the word – like an old bitch, Mr. Bunting, like an old bitch!'

# THE FIRST IRISH HARP
# SOCIETY AND BUNTING'S
# 1809 *COLLECTION*

In August 1808, Stephen White had placed a newspaper advertisement[75] suggesting that he intended to return to his native city, so book him now 'speedily' for tuning and repairs. The heading was 'Mr. White, organ builder, pianoforte & harp maker, from London'.

That reference to the harp was no coincidence for the savvy businessman. Earlier that year, on St Patrick's Day, the first Irish Harp Society was inaugurated with a subscription list 'of the Noblemen and Gentlemen associated for the purpose of reviving and encouraging the Irish harp'. It had been preceded by a carefully placed letter to the editor of the *Belfast News-Letter* on Friday 26 February 1808, page 2, and simply signed 'N'. It began:

> Sir, having some time ago learnt that a scheme was on foot for reviving the ancient music of our country, and thinking that the enclosed arguments in favour of it may induce some to lend their assistance, I offer it for your insertion. Yours, 'N.'

Then followed a lengthy piece with some key messages to tug at the heart strings and a call to action:

> Let a few, a very few years elapse, and this monument of our ancient civilisation, which so often added splendour to the hospitable halls of our ancestors, will disappear. For a length of time the profession of Bard

has been confined to a part of the community who generally experience all the wretchedness of poverty; a few blind harpers are now the only remains of our numerous bards. While these few are yet alive it is in our power to revive this nearly extinct art.

Music has been the principal resource of the blind, both for support and amusement. It appears that as their attention is not diverted by objects presented to another sense, they are peculiarly fitted to attain perfection in whatever is conveyed to their mind by sound. Some of the best poets and musicians that have ever appeared in the world, were men from whom the all-inspiring scenes of nature were shut out, ...

If, however, Music should not find a place among your pleasures, surely there is not a person in whom the sacred fire of Patriotism is so truly extinct that they do not feel the spirit of their fathers rise within them at the sound of the Harp, and sigh with regret that they have suffered the emblem of their country to remain so long neglected.

That was capped with the first stanza from the Sixth Canto of Sir Walter Scott's narrative poem *The Lay of the Last Minstrel* – 'Breathes there a man, with soul so dead ...'

With the 1808 St Patrick's Day meeting delivering a lengthy subscription list of 'Noblemen and Gentlemen', it's good to see the two prolific Belfast letter writers, Martha McTier and Mary Ann McCracken, amongst the small handful of women who are listed. Many names already encountered in these pages were on the list, including Edward Bunting of course, two McCracken brothers (John jun. and Francis), Henry Joy, Thomas Hull, Drs James McDonnell and Robert Tennent. There were 191 names in total – a really healthy beginning.

McDonnell had apparently repaired relationships with some people after the Russell reward fiasco in 1803. He and Tennent now produced a statement for the press to explain to the public the progress and views of the new institution. [76]

... [The society's subscription funding is] for the instruction of a select number of pupils on the Irish Harp, and have engaged Mr. Arthur O'Neill as teacher — a man whose character and talents qualify him highly for the employment. It is proposed to select twelve or more persons, of either sex, from such candidates as offer, without distinction of sect or country; and the Society call upon all who delight in the national music, and are fond of contemplating those remains of Ireland, which bespeak the possession of science and civilization in periods of remote antiquity, to co-operate with them in this design. It is hoped that search will be made, especially among the habitations of the poor, for such persons as seem to be highly endowed with natural musical talents, and who, from their age and dispositions, may appear most likely to succeed as scholars. It is hoped likewise, that such pecuniary aid will be contributed by the generous and enlightened, as shall enable the Society to extend their views beyond the mere business of tuition; by giving premiums and support to such of the pupils as are likely to attain eminence in their profession. ...

Down to business: A sub-committee of three was 'requested to receive an estimate from Mr. White for making three harps ...' The July 1808 meeting resolved 'that the three gentlemen appointed at the last meeting ... be further instructed to learn from him the lowest terms on which he would agree to furnish that number or a single harp on the plainest pattern and if he will engage one for 20 guineas or three for 12 or 15 guineas each[,] to make an agreement with him accordingly'. [77]

Two other potential harp-makers had also been approached: Mr McClenaghan and Mr McCabe. The first was never heard from again, the second delivered a specimen of his work but the committee was unimpressed. Mr. McCabe was informed 'that they will give five guineas for the harp and if he refuse to sell it at that price, they will give one guinea for the loan they have had of it.'

The Society seemed to be well organised and its minute book for the first two and a half years survives in the Beath Collection in the Linen Hall Library. The hand-writing itself, as much as the content, charts a trajectory from neat business-like organisation to increasing desperation as funding becomes more and more difficult.

At the beginning of August, Bunting chaired a meeting of the Society and 'in consequence of his observations' the meeting was adjourned for a month to allow time for Drs Tennent, McDonnell and Bryson 'to draw up rules and regulations for the better governance of the Society'. These would include fines for late arrival and larger fines for non-attendance.

It's good to find Bunting so involved in the new Society's work, even as he sought to bring his next *Collection* to publication. On 12 August 1808 he wrote to Dr Charles Burney, the now 82-year-old music historian, with a series of questions, including 'From whence do you conceive that Ireland had its harp in any form, and when did it take its present one?' He needed answers in a hurry: 'I have to request that any communication you are kindly inclined to make, may be soon as the work in question is in forwardness for the press.'[78]

Just over a week later, Bunting sent a 'Prospectus' to the newspapers entitled *The Entire of* The Ancient Melodies of Ireland, *adapted to the piano forte, by Edward Bunting, now nearly ready for publication.*[79]

It described the work's contents, mentioning original songs in their native language with prose translations; several of the finest airs arranged for voice with instrumental accompaniment and with English words 'prepared by gentlemen of acknowledged poetical talents'. There would be an old Irish lesson and prelude, played for several generations, and latterly, by Denis Hempson, the Harper of Magilligan, 'from whom it was taken down shortly before his decease'. (Hempson had died in November 1807, said to have been 112 years old.)

There would also be an original melody, or recitative, which Bunting had discovered 'sung in artless strains by the aborigines of different parts of Ireland, to Ossianic poems'.

There would be 'An Extensive Memoir on the Harp'. Other subjects would include the principles of how the Irish Harp is tuned and played, its relationship to ancient instruments, musical terms in Irish, 'and an inquiry into the Highland and Lowland music of Scotland; with an historical account of the Bagpipe'.

There would be four engraved plates, and all would be contained in 'two volumes folio, and an octavo volume, with elegant engravings to elucidate different parts of the subject'.

Subscriptions would be received at all the principal music shops in the United Kingdom and by the booksellers in Belfast.

The price of the first volume, One Guinea – of the second, fifteen shillings British; one half paid at subscribing for either volume, or for the entire work. Each volume a Crown additional to non-subscribers.

Subscribers' names to be printed, and a copious table of contents. The extent of the Impression will be governed by the subscriptions; early applications are therefore required.

Belfast, August 20, 1808.

Late in August and into September, Bunting travelled in Armagh, Fermanagh, Sligo, Dublin (where he inspected and measured 'Brian Borhoim's' harp), his brother's in Drogheda, back to Dublin, on to Limerick and then home via Drogheda again. Writing to Mary Ann on 10 September 1808 from Dublin:[80]

> I got some curious airs from the people in the neighbourhood of Sligo ... but I met with very few tunes indeed, that I had not before.

Again on 21 September 1808, from Dublin to Mary Ann:[81]

> ...I have got three tunes, one of which Cody, the piper, calls 'O'More, King of Leix's March,' and two others, viz. 'The Cavalcade of the O'Neils,' and 'The March of Owen Roe O'Neil'. I am anxious to have everything done in the best manner. I have gone too far to recede, otherwise I should, from the difficulty of the undertaking, give it up altogether. I think Miss Balfour's 'Fairy Queen' very good. The 'Fairy Queen' of Carolan, however, was not intended by him for words, but as a piece of music for the harp; therefore, it would not answer to have it now set with words. These some days past I have been running after an old woman named Betty Walsh, whom I have seen once before, and heard her play. It is possible I may pick up some airs from her. I have been making every exertion to find out her residence. I intend setting off for Limerick to-morrow eve, ... at any rate, I have got one material part finished, that of the technical terms, etc., with their roots and translations, which we could not do without for the memoir.

At the Harp Society's six-monthly general meeting in November 1808, 'Edward Bunting, William Magee and John McCracken jun. were appointed to examine and investigate the talents and qualifications of the boys already on the list and how to be hereafter proposed as pupils'. An advertisement was placed in the press calling on subscribers to pay their subscriptions and inviting the public to assist the institution. That initial enthusiasm was already proving difficult to maintain.

Fortunately Stephen White had not yet returned to London, despite his earlier threat!

> Two harps, the workmanship of an ingenious mechanic in this town, were exhibited at the [Society's committee] meeting; and we are informed that several more are now making by the artist who has built two organs in this town, and will be ready for exhibition at the next meeting. [82]

At the committee meeting on 7 March 1809, 'Surgeon [Alexander] McDonnell proposed, and Alexander Mitchell seconded, that the Society do propose to use their influence in promoting a school for teaching the Irish language and encouraging James Cody as a Master for that purpose and that the secretary takes down in our books the names of such persons as mean to become scholars ...'

Cody was already being employed by Bunting to collect airs and songs. Twelve members signed up immediately, including the Rev. Mr Groves and the Rev. Mr Drummond. Action followed. This was the notice on page 3 of the *Belfast News-Letter* on 11 July:

### IRISH HARP

THE PUBLIC are informed that a SCHOOL for teaching the IRISH LANGUAGE is now open under the patronage of the Society for preserving the knowledge of the Irish Harp.

Every necessary information respecting it, may be had at No. 8, Pottinger's-Entry, every day from 10 to 12 o'Clock.

EDWARD GROVES, Sec.

July 10, 1809.

It is requested that any person capable of giving any information relative to the ANCIENT NATIONAL MUSIC, or to MANUSCRIPTS in the IRISH LANGUAGE, will communicate it to the Secretary. Letters on the subject to be addressed to the Rev. EDW. GROVES, 22, Mill-street, Belfast.

No.8 Pottinger's-entry was the venue for the Society's committee meetings and it also had the designation of the 'Music Hall'. Cody used the Rev. William Neilson's *An Introduction to the Irish Language* (1808).

At that 7 March meeting it was also resolved that the members should dine together 'every Patrick's Day to celebrate the anniversary of the institution' and that intention should be 'published in the Belfast Papers'.

It's interesting how so much could be achieved in those years with very little notice. The dinner just ten days later was a great success. The room was ornamented with 'a transparency representing St. Patrick in his robes and crozier, and an allegorical figure of Hibernia, with her appropriate emblems ... In the centre of the room was suspended an ancient Irish Harp, decorated with garlands of shamrocks. The walls of the room were ornamented in a corresponding manner.'[83] And there was music.

The venerable harper, [Arthur] O'Neill, entertained the lovers of harmony with several national airs', then songs were sung before 'Mr. [James] Cody who has lately come from the West of Ireland, to assist in the collection of Irish melodies, performed some favourite airs on the pipes. As the glass enlivened by the toast, circulated, and the heart, alive to

71

the sensations excited, began to expand more freely, the meeting was gratified with an exhibition of a different and interesting nature.

Eight blind boys, supported, clothed, and instructed on the harp, by the Society, were admitted. This living proof of the good already resulting from their patriotic exertions, excited universal interest. They were received with repeated bursts of applause! After playing some airs, as a specimen of their progress, highly flattering to their aged teacher, they retired; and the company prepared for the usual routine of conviviality.

That conviviality included, as always, a multiplicity of toasts. Did Bunting take umbrage when toast no.10 was for his *bête noire*, 'Anacreon Moore', as Thomas Moore was known, while he, Bunting, was down at no.16 – 'the preserver of the remnant of our national music, and success to his publication'?

Bunting was missing from Society business for a long period after this because he had to be in London to oversee that publication. The March 1809 edition of the *Belfast Monthly Magazine* carried a 'hard-sell' piece for his forthcoming *Collection*.[84] Basically it was a reprinting of his 'Prospectus', preceded by this:

Mr. Bunting is at present in London superintending this long-expected collection, which is now *in the Press*, and will shortly be published with the highest embellishment of London Engravings. As the scope of this laborious undertaking, to which Mr. Bunting has devoted at least seventeen years, may not be known to some of your readers, the following account of it will be acceptable.

That paragraph was signed simply 'A Subscriber' (perhaps Bunting himself or maybe one of the magazine's proprietors: William Drennan, John Templeton (botanist and friend of the McCrackens) and John Hancock (merchant and former Quaker) – the first two were former United Irishmen and all three were interested in radical politics).

In Bunting's absence, the Society enlisted the help of a new musical figure in Belfast, Vincenzo Guerini from Naples, a teacher of Italian, violin, piano and singing, to assess the new harps by Stephen White. Of course, if Bunting had been around there would have been a conflict of interest!

In September 1809, it was decided to purchase White's harps at ten guineas each. More, it was resolved 'that the secretary write to the secretary of the Dublin Harp Society, to inform him that harps of superior tone can be procured here'.

So it must have been somewhat embarrassing when the *Belfast Commercial Chronicle* published a story about the Irish Harp the following month:[85]

> We understand that Mr. [John] Egan [of Dublin] has now finished an Irish Harp, which for ingenuity of construction, elegance of form, and sweetness of tone, are highly creditable to his talents. This Harp Mr. Egan intends as a patriotic present to the Charitable Institution of the [Dublin] 'Irish Harp Society'. On the sounding board at each side of the strings, in ancient characters, the following lines are inscribed, written we understand, by Matthew Weld Hartstonge, Esq.
>
> > The Harp once more at your command
> > With ancient song shall charm the land;
> > While each poor Blind, poor Orphan boy,
> > From your high bounty finds employ.
> > May Erin's Harp sweet peace prolong,
> > And glad inspire the dance and song!

The Dublin Society, inaugurated in July 1809, had been founded by John Bernard Trotter from Downpatrick, and employed the harper Patrick Quin from Portadown who had taken part in the 1792 Meeting in Belfast. That Society's rise and fall has been told elsewhere, but its existence did provoke a letter from 'Hibernicus' to the editor of the *Belfast Monthly Magazine*:[86]

SIR,

You will, doubtless, have observed with pleasure, that a Society has been formed in Dublin, for the exalted and patriotic purpose of reviving a knowledge of our ancient instrument, the Harp. Of the source from whence the idea originated, there can be but one opinion — that it was the *example of Belfast*; where a number of individuals, worthy of their country's name, had previously associated themselves together, and liberally subscribed for the same most interesting object.

Far be it from me to view the proceedings of the Dublin Harp Society with envy or jealousy. No; success attend their patriotic efforts, and unfading honour be their reward. May the spirits of our ancient bards hover o'er the regenerated strings of the Harp, and inspire the consecrated song of gratitude, swelling their praise in sweet and native strains. But, let it never be forgotten, that Belfast led the way — that from her bosom emanated the generous warmth which has recalled to animated existence the famed genius of Irish melody, so long, so shame-fully torpid. That in Belfast the first meeting of Irish harpers (procured by the inhabitants at considerable expense) took place in the year 1792. That Bunting of Belfast, whose musical talents are universally admired, was the first to rescue the fast fading reliques of our tuneful bards from threatening oblivion, and to give the world a complete collection, of celebrated and original Irish airs; and, finally, that the *first* Society for diffusing a knowledge of the Harp, and perpetuating our national music, was instituted in *Belfast*, a society that is entitled to the grateful tributes of Irishmen, and that I doubt not will be honourably recorded in the future annals of our country's taste, science, and glory.

Well dare anyone steal Belfast's thunder!

For Bunting, the months leading up to the actual publication of his second *Collection* were fraught. Rising to the challenge of the recent competition from Thomas Moore's *Irish Melodies*, Bunting had planned to have the Scottish poet Thomas Campbell write words, but in the end he had to settle for a few indifferent 'crumbs' from Campbell, bulked out by contributions from Miss

Mary Balfour (at whose school he taught) and single poems from Jonathan Swift, William Drennan and others.

With financial advice from Henry Joy (Mary Ann McCracken's cousin in Dublin); artistic and practical advice from John McCracken, jun., and probably Francis McCracken, about the plates (four engraved in total: an ancient Irish Harp in the possession of Noah Dalway Esq., Bellahill near Carrickfergus; a portrait of Hempson, the harper of Magilligan, County of L'Derry; and two plates of lyres, harps and bagpipes); along with some contributions about instruments from Mary Ann McCracken, it was gradually coming together.

In a letter to Francis (Frank) McCracken dated 26 April 1809, Bunting writes from the heart:

> ... for my part it is very nearly ready except that I have not got the songs from Campbell yet but all the other part is ready for engraving but I have not made up my mind how the arrangement is to be as to tunes and songs – never poor mortal regretted the loss of time which I have been about this business more than myself. It really has been a great, – aye, a monstrous loss, to me from first to last.

Writing from London to Mary Ann McCracken in October 1809, Bunting is poorly, both health-wise and financially:[87]

> I am far from being well at present, and this proceeds perhaps from my great anxiety about this work [the 1809 *Collection*]. For, as I must have during my long absence lost my business in Belfast, I have nothing to depend on but the sale of this work, for some time at least.

Many years later, Mary Ann recalled Bunting's strivings around this time:[88]

> ...[no] person now alive knows as much as myself, how completely he devoted many years of his life to the subject when his energies were all at their very best, and how frequently he went travelling through the country for many weeks at once, I think I may say months at one

time, attended by a Professor of the Irish Language [Patrick Lynch], at another by a musician [the piper James Cody], besides the entire summer of 1809 which he spent in London overseeing the publication of the work, all which was attended with considerable expense, besides the loss of time, which should otherwise have been occupied in giving instructions to others, so that I do not think he derived any pecuniary advantage from his publications.

It seems that Bunting's 1809 *Collection* wasn't available until January 1810. This was the advertisement on page 2 of London's *Morning Chronicle* on 20 January:

NEW MUSIC, published for the Author by CLEMENTI and Co. 26, Cheapside, Volume First of
A General COLLECTION of the ANCIENT MUSIC of IRELAND, arranged for the Pianoforte, and some of the most admired Melodies adapted for the Voice to Poetry, chiefly translated from the Original Irish Songs, by THOMAS CAMPBELL, Esq. and other eminent Poets. To the Work is prefixed an Historical and Critical Dissertation on the Egyptian, British and Irish Harp. The whole illustrated by elegant Engravings, by Edward Bunting. Price on Imperial £1. 11s. 6d. small size £1. 6s.

The *Collection* was received favourably, but Moore's *Irish Melodies* had taken off some of its shine. Bunting wrote to the London fashion magazine, *Le Beau Monde*, which had suggested that Moore and Stevenson's *Irish Melodies* was actually the first such collection and not Bunting's new volume. He reminded the editor of his '1796' *Collection*, pointing out that Sir John Stevenson (Moore's musician collaborator) had used 'no less than *eleven* of its airs in the first volume of his Melodies, which contained, in all, only *five* more'. He differentiated between Moore's *selection*, 'which an able musician could produce in his elbow chair', and his *collection*, 'with the advantage of having every well-authenticated, valuable, and really *ancient* melody that could be restored, by the active exertions of almost my lifetime – a Collection, which, at this period, it is out of the power of any other person to make'.

Bunting ended his letter by reporting that he was busily preparing his *second* Volume that 'independently of the mere music, it will contain (among other matter) a fund of original information, tending to throw light on the degree of improvement which Ireland must have attained in the art of Composition, at a very early period'.

Fashion and taste are fickle over time. Bunting's '1796', actually 1797, *Collection* was labelled Volume 1. So too was the 1809 Collection. Not a mistake, but a fresh start. The envisaged Volume 2 took over 30 years to come to fruition. By then, it was no longer Volume 2, but a new all-encompassing general collection. Each succeeding publication became less straightforward, the arrangements less simple, the introductory dissertations longer and learned. The truly positive outcome for Bunting's work is that his original notebooks remain to this day, readily accessible for study and research.

In 1811, Bunting entered into an agreement with the Dublin publisher Willis & Co., to reprint his latest Collection, presumably with the agreement of Clementi & Co. This rare edition was reprinted by the Linen Hall Library in 2012 to mark the 220th anniversary of the 1792 Harpers' Meeting.

# THE FIRST HARP SOCIETY CONTINUED

The suggestion that Bunting might have taken umbrage at the Belfast Harp Society's order of proposing toasts, placing Thomas Moore (aka 'Anacreon') six toasts ahead of Bunting on St Patrick's Day 1809, is possibly reinforced by a letter to the editor of the *Belfast News-Letter* a fortnight later. [89]

Corresponding to today's often venomous responses on social media, 'Urbanus' begins by complimenting the Harp Society. He'd read about its recent convivial meeting.

> ... Every friend of Ireland will rejoice to hear that our ancient music is revived, and that a Gentleman, well qualified for the task, is about to gratify the world with the publication of its most valuable remains. ...

Then the knives come out and the tirade begins:

> But it was not without a feeling of surprise, and of grief mingled with indignation, that I saw in the list of the toasts, dictated by the occasion, the name of an author, whose dissolute and licentious strains are a profanation to the harp of Erin. By what infatuation could a virtuous and public-spirited association, whose object is so truly patriotic and meritorious, profane the festival of our patron Saint, by crowning the bowl in honour of such a writer – a writer whose muse has ever been employed as the pander of vice, in conveying the most deleterious poison to the heart, and injuring and insulting the moral character and feelings

of his countrymen. I had hoped, Sir, that he had sunk into merited contempt and oblivion, and little suspected that Belfast would stretch forth a hand to pluck him from the gulf. Though ignorance and vanity have conspired to give him the name of *Anacreon*, the judicious critic, who knows how to reduce his overrated genius to its true level, can tell how little he is entitled to that appellation, ...

For many months after this outburst from 'Urbanus', Bunting was in London pursuing his business, arranging for Broadwood pianos to be sent to customers in Belfast and overseeing the finalising and publishing of his new *Collection*.

Based at 21 Cromac-street, the work of the Harp Society continued, with a new mission statement in November 1809.

This Society has been formed for the purpose of preserving the national music and national instrument of Ireland by instructing a number of blind children in playing the Irish harp and also for procuring and disseminating information relative to the language, history and antiquities of Ireland.

Three sub-committees were established, each of four members: one to collect subscriptions, inspect receipts and expenditure of the money and regulate the household economy; another to promote the knowledge of the Irish language and antiquities, and a third to superintend the musical progress of the pupils and to collect 'ancient music'.

The committee meeting on 5 December, perhaps to mark the new *Collection* and just maybe to build toasting bridges, decided to invite Bunting for a special dinner on Wednesday 20 December. A complimentary address was commissioned expressing the Society's gratitude for his exertions in rescuing the ancient airs from oblivion.

The dinner was well covered in the press. This next from the *Belfast News-Letter*:[90]

Sensible of the importance of his labours, and the ability with which he has accomplished the object of his pursuit, the Members of this Society determined, as a mark of individual respect and public esteem, to invite him to a splendid entertainment on Wednesday last. In the afternoon about fifty gentlemen received him with every mark of respect at O'Neil's Hotel. At five o'clock they sat down to a sumptuous dinner, elegantly served up, consisting of the choicest dishes with excellent wines.... After the cloth was removed, the bottle was freely circulated ...

Then came the toasts, interspersed with songs and a duet. Beginning with the King, the Army and Navy, and the memory of St Patrick, the tenth was to the Dublin Harp Society.

The chairman, Gilbert McIlveen, who had been a founding member of the United Irishmen, then proposed the toast to Bunting, 'the reviver of the ancient music of our country – and may his exertions be crowned with the success they merit.' The health of Mr Bunting was then 'drank with three times three'.

After a short 'thank you' reply, Bunting himself proposed a toast to the Harp Society of Belfast. More toasts followed, interspersed as before with songs. No mention of Anacreon.

Soon after dinner, O'Neil, the oldest Harper in Ireland, entered the room, followed by twelve pupils, one a female, all blind. The entrance of this reverend Patriarch and his juvenile charge, presented a scene truly impressive ... Being conducted to the middle of the room, they played several solos, duets, and trios ... Their performances gave much satisfaction, and it was very gratifying to behold this youthful group, the object of the Society's care, thus surrounded by their patrons, and delighting their ears with the music of ancient times.

The evening was spent in the most agreeable manner; and the glass, the toast, the song, and the sentiment, enlivened the hours, and protracted the festive scene till the morning was somewhat advanced. – *Rule Britannia* was then sung, the whole company joining in the chorus; after which they retired to their respective homes.

Over the next two months, the Society's committee agreed that two of the scholars, Edward McBride and Miss O'Reilly, 'in consequence of their service since their entrance into the Society', would be presented with a new set of clothes. The following list of the current scholars from the Society's minutes, was drawn up, 'stating age, from whence they came, by whom recommended, and when admitted into the Society'.

| | |
|---|---|
| *William Gorman* | *from Ballymena, Co. Antrim.* |
| | *aged 15; entered Society, June 1808* |
| | *recommended by Rev. John Fitzsimons* |
| | *of Ballymena* |
| | |
| *Patrick McGrath* | *from Dundalk, Co. Louth.* |
| | *aged 14; entered September 1808* |
| | *rec. by Mr Bell of Lambeg near Lisburn* |
| | |
| *Edward McBride* | *from Omagh, Co. Tyrone.* |
| | *aged 19; entered November 1808* |
| | *rec. by Mr Galbraith of Armagh* |
| | |
| *Patrick O'Neill* | *from near Dungannon, Co. Tyrone* |
| | *aged 13; entered January 1809* |
| | *rec. by Arthur O'Neill our Harper* |
| | |
| *James O'Neill* | *from Dungannon, Co. Tyrone* |
| | *aged 17; entered February 1809* |
| | *rec. by Dr James McDonnell, Vice President* |
| | |
| *Val. Rainey* | *of the Glens, Co. Antrim* |
| | *aged 14; entered February 1809* |
| | *rec. by the Vice President* |

*Abraham Wilkinson*      *of Ballymoney, Co. Antrim*
*aged 13; entered September 1809*
*rec. by Mr Moore of Moore's Lodge,*
*Co. Antrim*

*James McMolaghan*      *of Lifford, Co. Donegal*
*aged 13; entered October 1809*
*rec. by Mr Mitchell of Bier's Bridge [sic],*
*one of our committee*

*Bridget O'Reilly*      *from Virginia, Co. Cavan*
*[age not given]; entered September 1809*
*[rec. not listed].*

*Day Scholars not depending on the Society for support –*

*Edward O'Neill*    }
*Hugh Dornan*    }      *all of, or near, Belfast*
*John Wallace*    }

Not everything was sweetness and light. In February 1810, the committee had to investigate 'certain charges made by Arthur O'Neill our Harper against Bridget O'Reilly and Edward McBride, two of our Scholars, for having an improper connection. They [the committee members] were unanimously of [the] opinion that such Charges have been altogether groundless, false and unfounded.'

In May 1810, the music sub-committee 'was empowered to provide for and dispatch Ed McBride and Val Rainey to the country for three months in such a manner as shall most contribute to the business and honour of the Institution'. The sub-committee reported back one week later 'unable to report satisfactorily on the subject in consequence of a deficiency in Harps'. They were authorised to commission three new harps as soon as possible. Was Stephen White still in town?

By May 1810, the Society's funds were becoming worrying. Committee members were allocated specific Belfast streets to knock on doors and collect arrears and new subscriptions. Bunting was allocated Waring-street and Donegall Quay.

Other fund-raising included a Benefit Night at the Theatre, within the gift of its proprietor, Mr Montagu Talbot, who gave his permission for an evening on 15 June 1810. For their theatrical debut, the Scholars were each provided with 'a suit of Innisowen [sic] Blue Cloth', though after the event it was decided that 'the uniforms were to be locked away and only given out on public occasions'.

Money raised at the Benefit was used 'to pay some of the most pressing accounts'. Perhaps the situation was helped a little in June when James O'Neill and William Gorman were to 'be immediately dismissed [from] the Society as incapable by nature of learning the Harp'.

In July the committee discussed the propriety of allowing McBride and Rainey each 'to have a harp during the time they should be absent'. The sub-committee was authorised to use its discretion!

By September 1810 there were still no returns from those who had been nominated as collectors of subscriptions. The committee urged them to do their duty.

Things were not looking too good. Subscriptions were coming in too slowly and were inadequate to meet the Society's costs. A plan was agreed for a series of six Subscription Balls during the winter – gentlemen would pay $1\frac{1}{2}$ guineas for the season, and ladies 1 guinea. The Society's surviving minute book ends with the detailed regulations for those Balls.

This was the notice for the second of that season's balls:[91]

## IRISH HARP

THE SECOND SUBSCRIPTION BALL, for the Benefit of the pupils of the Irish Harp Society, will be held in the EXCHANGE ROOMS on TUESDAY the 8th of January, 1811 – Ladies to Draw for Places, and the Dancing to commence at NINE o'Clock.

No Person can be admitted but Subscribers, or such as have an extra Ticket. Strangers can be accommodated with extra Tickets, by applying to the Stewards.

It is requested, that those who attend the Balls, will appear in Irish Manufacture.

JOHN McCRACKEN, }
JAMES RAMSEY, } Stewards.

THOMAS HULL,
Master of the Ceremonies.

# THE FIRST HARP SOCIETY
# ENDS WITH A WHIMPER

In late May 1811, the *Belfast Commercial Chronicle* was commenting that the Society's 'funds stand in great need of the well-known liberality of the inhabitants of the town'.[92]

The subscription balls were maintained for two seasons, the last one on 16 April 1812. And that was presumably the real ending of the Society, even though it has always been said to have officially expired in 1813.

All was not at all well as revealed in a very lengthy letter to the *Belfast Commercial Chronicle*. A whistle-blower was at work.

The letter, 'to the Editor of the Belfast Chronicle', was entitled 'MR O'NEILL, THE IRISH MUSICIAN', and it is a wonderful piece of writing. There are some cuts here – and maybe there should be more – but this condemnatory outpouring is a job very well done:[93]

> SIR, – The last Minstrel of Erin, unfriended, exigent, and bent with years, claims the attention of the liberal and benevolent inhabitants of Belfast, in the language of *absolute necessity*. He came to our town possessed of, at least, something above immediate want, in a manner which reflected no dishonour on his former friends, his own propriety of conduct, nor on that respectable Society, which had made flattering overtures to him. Under the calm shade of their patronage and patriotism, he hoped to spend in evening sunshine, the close of a life full of incident and vicissitude. — The proposals made to him were worthy of his acceptance: therefore he became sole professor of *Ierne's* Lyre, in a kingdom where Irish minstrelsy had once flourished, but where a few,

faint struggles, would have composed its expiring soul for ever. The patriotic exertions of the BELFAST HARP SOCIETY were wafted on the wings of Fame, round the shores of the Old and New World — Europe, Asia, Africa, and America, heard and applauded our glorious National Institution; and their exalted panegyric, has long since re-echoed on the coastguarding rocks of Hibernia. Every Irish heart felt a new flame ...

... But, alas! a chilling frost fell on the warm spirit of the Institution, which damped its energies and relaxed its feelings. The glowing fire of their native emulation burned for a short time; and the noise which their undertaking made in the world, was kept aloof for a while, like the transitory reverberation of a sound among cliffs and rocks.

In a barbarous age, the blind bard of *Meles* was neglected by his countrymen, which Greece sorely repented after his death, when *Seven cities* contended for the honour of his birth. And, at a less enlightened period than the present, the merits of the sightless, but immortal MILTON, were but ill appreciated, when his Bookseller could not perceive the excellence of his *Paradise Lost*, or consider it of more worth than £15! — But these are not the dark days of HOMER, nor the purblind, inglorious times of the great Milton:— No; this is the unclouded age of Refinement, Literature, Philanthropy, and Philosophy, in which O'NEILL has the fortune to live. ...

... Alas! with all those advantages on his behalf — disappointed O'NEILL, the Irish Apollo in musical skill — Erin's *Amphion* in the captivating Lyric art, and the wire-waking *Orpheus* of Ireland, is neglected in the *very town* where *his* hopes and *our* expectations have been most highly raised. What is his situation at present?

Reader! condescend to follow me in fancy, and I will take the liberty of shewing you: Behold the venerable Minstrel, with age-silvered head, whereof Time has reaped a partial harvest — with brows, furrowed with the cares and perplexities of *seventy-three years*, sitting in his wretched dwelling of smoke, in a filthy lane off Mill-street, where all the inclemencies of the weather may enter, sooner than a ray of sunshine; but of the latter, he neither does nor has reason to complain. Fix your eyes of sympathy on the forlorn Bard, as he sits shivering in his cold region of poverty, leaning over the silent companion of his journey through life; the soother of his misfortunes, and sighing for the years that are gone, and the light featured joys of other days, which have long since rolled away on the stream of Time. Members of *The Harp Society*, I will not reflect on your conduct, however unseemly it may appear; but, in candour, I must say that, as your townsman, I am mortified in feelings, and astonished at the way you have treated the *aged professor*.

You were, at first, considered a respectable society, composed of virtuosos — amateurs — men of classic taste and classic knowledge — with a northern Nobleman for your President, and an Antiquarian and profound Philosopher for your Vice-President. Besides, your Institution must have been established on a tolerably good basis, when you could hold out such flattering hopes to O'NEILL, and enter into a regular and legal contract with him, that he should receive £60 *per annum*, for the exercise of his professional knowledge, without limitation of time: it is supposed you included the remaining years of his life, and that you must have even considered them too few to effectuate the glorious purpose of reviving the Harp. What part, or how much of this salary he has received I know not; but I understand from what should be thought *correct information*, that you are his debtor in no less than £160! therefore he could not have received very much; and truly, this sum should purchase you immortal fame! —

He is no longer employed: why so? Because he has not a *single pupil* for instruction. The inhabitants of other towns have said that the conspicuous and ruling features of your character were pride, ostentation, vanity, and love of fame that could be purchased at a very cheap rate, or at no expense: let me intreat you to persuade them, at least for once, that they have spoken from misinformation or false judgment, by adopting a contrary and more becoming mode of behaviour — conduct more worthy of yourselves and our approvance, on this sublime occasion. Be assured, the Minstrel of Erin is about to leave you — and with contrary ideas of your honour and integrity to those he indulged when coming to Belfast — do not suffer *three weeks* to elapse, or you will lose sight of him, and perhaps never again behold him. ...

And you ye bountiful inhabitants of Belfast, let me touch the chords of your soft sympathy —the wires of your gentle fellow-feeling for the necessitous Minstrel. The silent, uncomplaining O'NEILL, a man worthy of better times, is at present not only friendless, but without pecuniary means to procure subsistence! His craving necessities, I know, would urge him to become a debtor for the common necessaries of life; but who, oh inhabitant of Belfast! will be willing to credit abject poverty?

Alas; you will say, 'too few if any!' Reflect how awkwardly and unpleasantly he is situated; living, no! half-starving in a cold, damp, smoky house, where the *Asthma* is preying like a ravenous vulture on his decayed lungs. Hereditary and national pride forbids him to disclose his distressing tale, or let his wants be known — his manly spirit dies within him, when he thinks of acknowledging his extreme poverty. He has never told me of his wants, yet I have guessed at and know them — for a true-born O'NEILL would be equally as reluctant to say he was hungry as to acknowledge he was conquered! ...

The letter, written in Belfast is dated 25 November 1812 and signed AUGUSTUS. He had previously written to the same paper on Saturday 7 November (page 4) in a 'Letter addressed to the Belfast Harp Society respecting their conduct towards Mr O'Neil [sic] the Professor of Irish Music'. Augustus's hand-writing must have been difficult to decipher – that first letter had several misinterpreted words which were corrected in the following Monday's newspaper. This from June 1813:[94]

### IRISH HARP

It is with pleasure we observe, in the Theatrical department of this day's publication, that Mr Talbot has generously given the use of the Theatre on Wednesday evening, for a benefit to this Institution, which has latterly been in a languid situation, in consequence of the funds being inadequate to its support.

The Pupils, we understand, were, some time ago, sent into the country, to provide for themselves till the establishment be renovated; when they will be recalled to prosecute their education under their venerable tutor, and to acquire a knowledge of the principles of the art, agreeably to the modern practice, which will be done by introducing an improvement on this instrument similar to the pedal Harp, without impairing the original melody.

We think it worthy of notice at this time, that Belfast has the credit of being the first, indeed we may say the only place in the kingdom, that, in the nineteenth century, has recovered a great portion of our national music, so universally admired; and has acquired a distinguished honour by rescuing a favourite instrument from that oblivion to which, in all probability, it was otherwise doomed.

It will, therefore, be highly creditable to the town to support it on the present occasion, and enable the Committee to lay a favourable statement of the establishment before the public.

The messaging may have been intentionally more upbeat than the reality. Belfast's first Irish Harp Society had been doomed the previous year and never recovered. The languid situation became terminal; too little support was forthcoming from the town; the funds ran out. It closed formally in 1813 with not even a death notice in the papers.

A January 1816 announcement and programme listing[95] for a Grand Concert in Dublin's Clarendon-street Chapel 'under the direction of Dr Cogan' includes 'Between the two Parts, a Duo on Irish Harps, by Messrs Rennie [Rainey] and MacBride [sic], from the Belfast Irish Harp Society, being their first appearance in Dublin.' The concert was 'to liquidate the vast expenditure incurred in the repairs of, and improving the avenues leading to the Chapel.'

As for the Society's Master, Arthur O'Neill, the standard story is that he 'was paid an annual annuity of £30 for life by his friends', all or part of it said to have been arranged by Dr McDonnell. It clearly wasn't enough. In May 1814 he persuaded Mr Talbot to hold a benefit for him:[96]

O'Neill, the Irish Harper, respectfully announces to the inhabitants of Belfast, that several of his friends have suggested to him, as the means of extricating himself out of distress to try a benefit at the Theatre; and Mr Talbot having kindly consented, this evening will be performed, the celebrated Comedy of *The Heir at Law*.

Then followed this, nearly two years later, from the *Belfast News-Letter* in March 1816:[97]

The concert for the benefit of ARTHUR O'NEILL, the Irish Harper, will be held in the Exchange Rooms tomorrow evening; we have seen the bill of the performance, which promises an entertainment calculated to gratify those possessed of the nicest musical talent, and so varied, as to render it pleasing to persons of every taste.

The arrangements have been made by Mr. Hewett of the Theatre, who has been very assiduous to render the performance interesting and worthy of public attention. Mr. Hare will play some of the most favourite airs on the musical glasses, and we rejoice to find, that all the persons who have so kindly and generously come forward to relieve an aged and infirm man, deprived of sight and destitute of every earthly comfort, have shewn a meritorious desire to render themselves as useful as possible; from such exertions we anticipate a benefit which will produce a sum worthy the occasion.

Books containing the songs, etc., to be sung and played, will be sold at the door at $2\frac{1}{2}$d. each. The performance commences precisely at a quarter before eight o'clock, the door will open at six.

Hopefully it was a success, for eight months later, came this:[98]

A few days ago, at Maydown in the county of Armagh, Mr. Arthur O'Neill, professor of the Irish harp [died] at the advanced age of 90 years. O'Neill was a pleasing companion, full of anecdote and historic information. He was a perfect reservoir of the ancient Irish harmony.

Many of our national airs would have been lost but for his retentive memory and pure and taste. His performance on the harp was unrivalled, but he adhered tenaciously to the genuine style and simple taste of the Irish musical compositions, rejecting with disdain the corrupt adscititious ornament with which it has been loaded by modern performers. Like Ossian, Carolan and Stanley, he was blind. In Irish genealogy, in heraldry, and in bardic lore, O'Neill was pre-eminent. He was better than all this – 'an honest worthy man'. There is an excellent portrait of O'Neill in Mr. Bunting's valuable collection of Irish airs'

And where was Bunting during all this? He was earning his living, teaching, demonstrating and selling pianos (he was said to be an especial favourite at Broadwood's piano company in London). In 1813 he organised Belfast's first-ever Music Festival for charity along the lines of those in England. Like the big regional English festivals, Bunting's Festival was anchored by performances of Handel's *Messiah* (its first near-complete performance in Belfast) and Haydn's *Creation*.

In 1812, Dr John Gamble, on one of his several visits to the north of Ireland commented on Belfast's musical life. [99]

Music was the favourite recreation in Belfast and many were no mean proficients in it. They are probably indebted for this to Mr. Bunting, a man well known in the musical world.

He has an extensive school here and is organist to one of the meeting-houses; for so little fanaticism have now the Presbyterians of Belfast, that they have admitted organs into their places of worship. At no very distant period this would have been reckoned as high a profanation as to have erected a crucifix.

I was highly gratified with Mr. Bunting's execution on the piano-forte. Mr. Bunting is a large, jolly-looking man; that he should fail to be so is hardly possible, for Belfast concerts are never mere music meetings – they are always followed by a supper and store of wine and punch.

Mr. Bunting is accused of being at times capricious, and unwilling to gratify curiosity. But musicians, poets and ladies have ever been privileged to be so.

In 1815 Bunting travelled to the near continent, taking in Paris where George Petrie said he played his Irish airs to 'many of the most eminent musicians'. Petrie continued: [100]

> Led by his love for music and particularly of the organ, which was at all times his favourite instrument, he passed from France into Belgium where, from the organists of the great instruments at Antwerp and Haarlem, he acquired much knowledge, which it was our good fortune to have often heard him display on our own organ at St. Patrick's [Dublin].

Bunting had fallen out with the Second Presbyterian Church in 1817 and he now moved to the recently built St George's Church of Ireland in High Street with its temporary Stephen White organ, the one formerly belonging to Thomas Hull and probably his ballroom. [101]

Belfast nearly loses sight of Bunting in 1819 when he married at the tender age of 46. His bride was Miss Mary Anne Chapman, daughter of the lady principal of a Belfast school. Just prior to the engagement, Mary Anne's mother took up a new post in Dublin, and thither the newly-weds went to live.

# THE SECOND BELFAST
# IRISH HARP SOCIETY

The bad press linked to the treatment of Arthur O'Neill, including the letters and the notices of his benefit concerts, eventually reached Calcutta in India. There, an Ulsterman John Williamson Fulton, created a fund 'which has been principally collected by his exertion, and to which he is a large contributor,' for the revival of Irish Music, but also to 'afford assistance to the blind and helpless'. [102]

The contributors were predominantly from Ireland and mainly from the north. An early collaborator in the new subscription was Alexander Gordon Caulfield who drowned while crossing the Ganges not long after the fund had been established. 'It is a remarkable instance of regard for the memory of that gentleman, and zeal for the measure, that a few of his Irish friends instantly subscribed a sum for the payment of his *annual* contribution – *in perpetuity*.

Fifteen men, and they were all men, met in Belfast on 16 April 1819 to constitute a Society for the Management of a Fund formed in India, 'to revive the HARP and ANCIENT MUSIC of IRELAND'. Thomas Verner was in the chair and the others included names well-known from the first Harp Society – Henry Joy, William Tennent, John McCracken, Edward Bunting, John Templeton, etc.

John Williamson Fulton had been in correspondence with Henry Joy and Robert Williamson 'on the subject of the benevolent, liberal, and patriotic views of the Subscribers in India, whose donations and subscriptions form the Fund'. The donations, raised from 309 subscribers, of whom more than half were army officers, [103] dated back at least to 17 March 1818 when it was noted that preceding remittances from Mr Fulton had been handed to Joy and Williamson 'through another channel'. So the India fund likely dates back to 1817.

The meeting reported that the total of the Fund at that stage was £1,079. 16s. 0d British, negotiated to £1,192 3s. 2d. Irish. The new Irish Harp Society then created a lengthy list of 'Original Members' with a clause that deemed original members would also include (i) donors and annual subscribers in India upon their return to Ireland, and (ii) surviving Members of the Belfast Harp Committee of the year 1792, not already included on the list.

Item xi on the business stated

> That Mr. Edward Bunting be requested to order three Harps to be made on the most improved construction, in order that an adequate number may be purchased, if those shall be approved of. That Mr. Bunting be also requested to ascertain what Harpers are to be found, competent to the tuition of a number of pupils, and the terms on which such teacher or teachers can be had.

Ten years had passed since Bunting's 1809 *Collection*. The local press – and others – piled the pressure on Bunting. Reports of the 16 April meeting came with this health warning: [104]

> It is now more desirable than ever, that the collection of *Additional Airs*, made by Mr. Bunting, several years ago, with unprecedented labour and success, should be speedily published; with them the public would be in possession of a complete body of the Ancient Melodies of the country. It is certain that several of those not yet published are equal to the finest that have ever appeared: without them every former collection, in this kingdom, is incomplete.

With his wedding only a week away, Bunting reported back to the committee on 13 September. It was reported in the *Belfast News-Letter*:

On Monday the 13th inst. a meeting was held of THE ULSTER HARP SOCIETY, at Belfast, when three elegant Harps, made by Mr. Egan, of Dublin, were produced by Mr. Edward Bunting, and greatly approved of. The tone appears stronger than in the common instrument, and by a simple contrivance alterations in the key are produced without delay. This is the principal improvement, and it was much wanted. Nothing is now required to bring into effect the objects of the liberal founders of this Society *in India* but *an experienced Harper*, of good morals, and competent to the tuition of a number of pupils. He must be master of the ancient Melodies of Ireland and acquainted with the comparatively modern compositions of Connollan and Carolan. Such a person would be well accommodated, and find it [in] his interest to settle in Belfast.

The proprietors of newspapers in the four provinces of Ireland might contribute to this purpose by having the goodness to copy this paragraph into their prints.

There was a considerable time delay in the information exchange between Belfast and Bengal, for obvious reasons in those days. The *Bombay Gazette* for 15 September 1819 has this: [105]

Extract of a letter from Belfast, of the 17th December, 1818, to the Managers of the subscription in Bengal, for the extension and preservation of the Harp and Music of Ireland.

We beg leave to acknowledge the receipt of the very liberal remittances from India, through your hands, on account of the revival of the Irish Harp, the particular document of which is subjoined. We have delayed addressing you as we now do, till we could inform you of our progress in carrying your wishes into execution. It is favourable to an undertaking so interesting to Irishmen, that so much has been already effected in recovering the strains of our ancient Bards, as a great deal of our earliest and finest Music, which in the lapse of ages had been rarely listened to and seldom indeed to be heard, even in the remote part of Ireland: is now recorded in a printed form, or prepared ready for publication. Owing to the exertions of the Harp Societies, a number of blind musicians have been taught to perform and preserve our Irish Melodies and under one of the most severe privations, not only to support themselves, but from the cultivation of another sense, in some measure to minister as blind minstrels to the gratification of their countrymen. ...

Bunting's searches for a teacher continued: [106]

## A HARPER WANTED.

*For the Irish Harp Society, at Belfast.*
(Founded on the liberal Subscriptions of a number of Friends
of the Ancient Music of Ireland, in India)

HE must bear a good character, and be competent to the TUITION of a number of PUPILS.

– It is necessary that he be conversant with the Ancient Melodies of this Country, and the Compositions of CONNELLAN, CAROLAN, &c.

An adequate Annual Salary will be given; and a convenient Dwelling-House, with School-Rooms, provided.

Applications in person, or by post, from Harpers in the different Provinces of Ireland, to be made to EDWARD BUNTING, Esq., now settled in Dublin, (Leeson-street, No. 18); and to the Secretary of the Irish Harp Society, at Belfast.

The Society, sensible of the many years arduous and successful labours of Mr. BUNTING, in collecting the original Music of the Irish Harp, from its purest sources, request his speedily perfecting the work, by publishing the remainder of the Ancient Melodies; and that he continue to give that zealous attention in *Dublin*, to the objects of the Irish Harp Society, which he has done during his residence at *Belfast*.

Signed by order,

JOHN WARD, Secretary.

Belfast, September, 23, 1819

The appointment was none other than Edward McBride from the first Harp Society at a salary of £40 per annum. The Society's rules specified a total of four boarding students and a maximum study of two years. Provided the student was of good conduct and deemed to be proficient on the harp, the Society would present them with a harp, complete with the student's name engraved on a brass plate.

By August 1821 the Society was responsible for four resident pupils: Patrick Byrne (blind), Co. Meath, aged 23; Thomas Hanna, Antrim, aged 18; Patrick McCloskey (blind), Banbridge, aged 12; Jane McArthur (blind), Ballycastle, aged 17. In addition, there were two day pupils: Hamilton Graham, aged 18, and Hugh Frazer, aged 13. [107]

Of these, we know that Patrick Byrne completed his studies in May 1822 and was presented with a John Egan harp. He enjoyed the patronage of Evelyn John Shirley of Lough Fea House, Magheracloone, Co. Monaghan, and after Belfast he went on to enjoy a very successful career across these islands. In January 1841, at Buckingham Palace, he was appointed Irish Harper to HRH Prince Albert and two days later he played for Queen Victoria.

Bunting penned him a reference in 1840 which included these glowing comments: [108]

> ... when playing those sweet melodies ... in that extremely soft and whispering manner which can perhaps be best executed by the delicately sensitive touch of a person deprived of sight ... as also that in which you stop the vibrations of the strings ... you being able to accompany with your voice those primitive airs in the words of their native language ...

Another of the 1821 harpers, Patrick McCloskey died in June 1826, aged 19. His headstone in Kilrush graveyard, Lisburn, was erected by the Irish Harp Society, 'in memory of their pupil, Patrick McCloskey, in consideration of his good conduct and proficiency in music'. [109]

In August 1821, George IV visited the Mansion House in Dublin when four Irish harpers played for him. They were McBride, Rainey, James MacMonagal (likely the same as James McMolaghan from the first Harp School) and John

MacLoghlin, also said to be from the Belfast School.[110]

In January 1822, McBride was succeeded in Belfast by Valentine Rainey (sometimes Rennie or Reanney or other variations).

> He has permission, out of hours, to attend Ladies and Gentlemen for tuition on the Irish and Pedal Harp; and also, to play in genteel families in the evenings. The Irish Harp, in his hands, will be found so superior to what musical persons have been accustomed, that the committee take the liberty to recommend him to the notice of musical amateurs[111]

Rainey was 42 when he died 'after a lingering illness' and the *Belfast News-Letter* published a fulsome tribute to him.[112] He was from Cushendall, Co. Antrim and, 'by his father's side', he was a second cousin to the poet Robert Burns. He was a good violinist at the age of eleven, but his passion was the Irish Harp. Thanks to Dr McDonnell, 'who was forcibly struck by his genius', he was able to study with Arthur O'Neill in Belfast.

> So well established and so extensive was his fame, that a Society of Irishmen resident in the East Indies had fixed upon him to go out to that country on liberal terms, for the purpose of introducing the Irish Harp into the East; but this flattering offer he ultimately declined, preferring to remain in his native country, ... he has left a widow and an only son – a boy aged six years and six months. ... he was interred in Friar's Bush burying ground.

The invitation to the East Indies, according to Bunting, was from the King of Oude. He relates how it was the Society which wouldn't part with Rainey, but that they sent out a piper with a new set of pipes to the East Indies instead. Unfortunately, one day *en route* to His Highness's palace, the piper fell off the boat while playing his pipes and drowned in the Ganges.

The first Harp School had its premises in Cromac-street and the second School was also based there up to around 1830. Shortly after Rainey's death, it moved to Talbot Street.

Not for long. Rainey was succeeded by James Jackson, who had been a pupil of Rainey. Unfortunately, at that point the money from India dried up. John Williamson Fulton had died in 1830 and without his drive and enthusiasm, the scheme fizzled out.

The Society's secretary made one last attempt to rejuvenate things. He wrote to potential friends of the Society on 10 October 1837: [113]

> ... For a number of years back, the state of Mr [Rainey's] Rennie's health prevented him paying the necessary attention to the musical education of the blind boys under his care, which, to a certain extent, affected the utility of this interesting charitable establishment.
>
> At the late meeting of Committee it was suggested, that this was a favourable opportunity for regenerating the Society, by giving the management to a new and younger class of our citizens; and as there are several harpers in the country who have acquired great proficiency by experience and travelling, the Society cannot be at a loss for a Teacher. It was therefore resolved —
>
> That as these funds were originally raised for the purpose of extending the cultivation and keeping alive the Irish Harp, it is imperative that this balance shall be applied to the same object, and if any individuals may hereafter offer their services for the attainment of that object, and be appointed, the said balance shall be so appropriated under their direction; and that, in the meantime, the House, Furniture, and Harps shall remain at their disposal ...

The attempt to raise interest and funds locally was unsuccessful.

John McAdam, the Society's secretary, depressingly updated Bunting in July 1839: [114]

> ... I am sorry to inform you that the funds [of the Harp Society] will be exhausted about the first of February next. After the first of August, we shall have only two boys; we are anxious to prolong the time, that one of the boys (William Murphy) may have as much instruction as can be

afforded, he having his eyesight perfect, and a natural taste for music. We were most desirous to have one Irish harper who could read music and thereby keep alive, for some time longer, a number of those national airs which so far as the Irish harp is concerned, were about to be lost for ever.

I mentioned to you that we might probably keep up the society for a few years longer by private subscription, but from the fact that the young harpers can only earn their bread by playing in hotels, where they are too liable to contract fatal habits, we think the money could be more usefully laid out in other charities.

Our gentry in Ireland are too scarce and too little national, to encourage itinerant harpers, as of old; besides, the taste and fashion of music no longer bears upon our national instrument: it had its day, but, like all other fashions, it must give way to novelty.

# BUNTING'S THIRD AND FINAL COLLECTION

Thirty years have passed by since Bunting's second *Collection*, 1809. He has had a busy career in Dublin as a businessman and organist. He has had a growing family of a boy (Anthony) and two girls. And yes, he has also been arranging many of the airs he'd gathered over the years.

Perhaps it was the letter from Dr McDonnell in Belfast, dated 26 October 1836, that finally spurred him into action:[115]

Dear Bunting,

You will not recollect my hand-writing, but I wish to bring to your recollection a subject we were speaking of when you were last here. It was about some songs or dirges.

I think you told me that you had gotten some of them which you had arranged and harmonised.

When you publish your music, which I now never expect to see, as I am so old and you so indolent, be sure to print some commentary upon the tunes stating all the conjectures that you can form about them ...

McDonnell did indeed live to see the final publication, dedicated to Queen Victoria, and with 100 pages of introductory material, including contributions from the young poet Samuel Ferguson and help from his wife Mary Anne and from George Petrie. There are notes about specific airs, 'an account of the old melodies of Ireland', titles in Irish and English, and 'a dissertation on the Irish harp and harpers.' The first *Collection* had 66 airs, the second 77. This 1840 collection has 151.

Gráinne Yeats has described the volume as 'large and elaborate', complaining that 'practically none of the airs can be played on the harp without extensive alteration, and the piano arrangements are made in a spirit so totally alien to traditional music, that they do not sound well even on the piano'.[116]

Bunting, of course, was not arranging the airs for the harp. His volume was aimed at his own bread and butter Broadwood piano market. Indeed George Petrie tells of how Bunting was a great favourite with the Broadwoods, 'so much so, that on his last visit to London, in 1839, they presented him with a grand piano-forte, which they allowed himself to choose out of their extensive manufactory'.

As John McAdam had understood, and as Bunting had probably understood a long time before this, the public interest had withered away to almost nothing. How delighted he would have been with the renewed interest in recent decades in the Irish Harp, in its performance practice, in Bunting's manuscript notebooks at Queen's University, Belfast, and in the contents of his historical reminiscences.

His life's work was complete and he was exhausted – as he told Mary Ann McCracken in a letter dated 9 May 1840:[117]

My labour at the Irish music is all but closed, which I am sure you are pleased to hear. My very last sheet is now printing off, and we expect to be able to publish in the course of a fortnight to the world. I begin to fear for the sale of it at last, for hitherto I never doubted, but at least we should sell as many in the course of six months as would pay the cost of publication. It now admits of doubt for many reasons; first, the taste for Irish music is on the wane, or rather weaned; and secondly, the price which we must make at £1. 10s. each book, stands much in the way of selling a great number. There are a few ardent lovers of their country whom I think will buy it, but, unfortunately, they are indeed few. We must hope the best, notwithstanding, but the work itself will remain a monument of my unwearied perseverance and industry for nearly fifty years, and I have the satisfaction of reflecting farther, that it could not at any period of the last thirty years have come out half so well, and with so much interest to both the antiquarian and the musician as at present. My discovery of the structure of Irish music, etc., in your house stamps the work with no common interest, which discovery makes the book invaluable. As a celebrated antiquarian here said, now any one may compose Irish tunes.

I have no hopes of its being of benefit to me or my family, the only remuneration I expect is a sort of introduction for Anthony, as the son of a man who toiled so long at the expense of both money, labour, and health. This last I add as I truly think it has in some degree shortened my stay in this world, in trying to restore (as poor Henry Joy said) a page in the history of man. What will that serve me when I shall be asleep in the grave, and very possibly be there before the fatiguing business appears. I may never see it.

He did live to see it – but not for long. Edward Bunting died on 21 December 1843 and is buried at Mount St Jerome Cemetery, Dublin.

[1] Giraldus Cambrensis, *Topographia Hiberniae*, c.1188, translated by Thomas Forester, revised and edited by Thomas Wright (In parentheses Publications, Medieval Latin Series, Cambridge, Ontario 2000), Distinction III, Chapter XI, p.71.

[2] *Belfast News-Letter*, Friday 19 November 1762, p.2

[3] *Belfast News-Letter*, Friday 5 October 1764, p.2

[4] *Belfast-News-Letter*, Tuesday 10 July 1792, p.3

[5] Edward Bunting, *The Ancient Music of Ireland, arranged for the Pianoforte. To which is prefixed a dissertation on the Irish Harp and Harpers, including an account of the old melodies of Ireland*, Dublin, 1840, p.78

[6] *Dublin Evening Post*, Saturday, 12 June 1784, p.1, also Tuesday 22 June, p.2

[7] Rev. Patrick Rogers, *The Irish Volunteers and Catholic Emancipation 1778-1793: A Neglected Phase of Ireland's History*, London 1934, p.247

[8] Peter Tuite, *Tuite Family* http://www.tuites1.com/442920037 (accessed 01 May 2022)

[9] Kat Dalglish, *Christopher MacEvoy* [sic] *of St Croix, Copenhagen and London* – A family of planters, merchants and slave-traders https://answersonapostcard.weebly.com/answers-on-a-postcard/category/slavery (accessed 01 May 2022)

[10] Orla Power, 'Irish planters, Atlantic merchants: the development of St. Croix, Danish West Indies, 1750–1766', (PhD thesis, NUI Galway, 2011), p.190.

[11] Roger Courtney, *Dissenting Voices: Rediscovering the Irish Progressive Presbyterian Tradition*, Ulster Historical Foundation, Belfast, 2013, p.63.

[12] The Special Collection department of Queen's University Belfast houses the Bunting Collection which includes an initial draft of O'Neill's Memoirs at MS 4/46

https://digital-library.qub.ac.uk/digital/collection/p15979coll9/id/1947/rec/16

There's also a fair copy at MS 4/14/1.

https://digital-library.qub.ac.uk/digital/collection/p15979coll9/id/1673/

As to be expected, there are some little differences between the two copies. One of those is that harper Patrick Carr in the earlier version was amended to Patrick Kerr in the later version.

[13] Also in the *Dublin Evening Post* on Tuesday 21 June 1785, p.1 and Saturday 2 July, p.1

[14] *Freeman's Journal*, Tuesday, 25 April 1786, p.4. A paragraph in between seemingly unrelated anecdotes within a lengthy miscellany entitled *Postscript*.

[15] QUB Special Collections, QUB MS 4/14/2,

https://digital-library.qub.ac.uk/digital/collection/p15979coll9/id/1153

[16] Jonathan Jeffrey Wright, *The 'Natural Leaders' and their World: Politics, Culture and Society in Belfast, c.1801-1832*, Liverpool, 2012, p.68

[17] E. Courtney (ed.), *William Drennan: Selected Writings: The Irish Volunteers 1775-1790*, Belfast 1998, pp.176,177

[18] Ultán Gillen, 'Irish Revolutionaries and the French Revolution'. *The Routledge Companion to the French Revolution and World History*. London, 2015, pp.8-14

https://research.tees.ac.uk/ws/files/6460530/560958.pdf (accessed 14 May 2022)

[19] Fergus Whelan, *May Tyrants Tremble: The Life of William Drennan*, 1754–1820, Dublin, 2020, p.70

[20] Mary Louise O'Donnell, 'A Driving Image of Revolution: The Irish Harp and its Utopian Space in the Eighteenth Century', *Utopian Studies*, vol.21, no.2, 2010, p.263

[21] Linen Hall Library, Beath Collection, IR/BEA/Box 3 (7)

[22] *Belfast News-Letter*, Tuesday, 13 December 1791, p.4

[23] John Gray, *The Sans Culottes of Belfast*, Belfast 1998, pp.12-27

[24] *Belfast News-Letter*, Tuesday, 24 April 1792, p.3

[25] *Northern Star*, Wednesday 18 July 1792, p.3

[26] *Belfast News-Letter*, Tuesday, 24 April 1792, p.3

[27] *Belfast News-Letter*, Tuesday, 10 July 1792, p.3

[28] Fergus Whelan, *May Tyrants Tremble*, p.98

[29] *Northern Star*, Saturday 7 July 1792, p.4

[30] *Northern Star*, Wednesday 11 July 1792, p.3

[31] T.W. Moody, R.B. McDowell and C.J. Woods (eds.), *The writings of Theobald Wolfe Tone*, 1763-98, Oxford, 1998, vol.1, pp.207-214

[32] William Theobald Wolfe Tone (ed.), *Memoirs of Theobald Wolfe Tone*, London, 1827, vol.2, p.232

[33] Gillian O'Brien, 'Spirit, impartiality and independence: *The Northern Star*, 1792–1797', *Eighteenth-Century Ireland / Iris an Dá Chultúr*, vol.13, 1988, p.23

[34] Edward Bunting, *The Ancient Music of Ireland*, 1840, p.73

[35] Edward Bunting, *The Ancient Music of Ireland*, 1840, p.63

[36] Don Johnston, 'Gaelic-Speaking Presbyterian Ministers of Dundalk/Ballymascanlan.' *Journal of the County Louth Archaeological and Historical Society*, vol.28, no.1 (2013), pp.64-67

[37]In a letter from Dublin to Mary Ann McCracken, dated 27 December 1827, Bunting refers to being 12 years old at his first introduction into the McCracken/Joy family.

[38]*Belfast News-Letter*, Tuesday, 24 November 1789, p.3. Advertisement dated 26 Nov.1789.

[39]'P' (aka George Petrie), 'Our Portrait Gallery, No.XLI', *Dublin University Magazine*, vol.29, no.169, January 1847, p.67; also at https://www.byersmusic.com/edward-bunting.php

[40]*Northern Star*, Wednesday 18 July 1792, p.3

[41]Edward Bunting, *The Ancient Music of Ireland*, 1840, p.65

[42]*Belfast News-Letter*, Tuesday, 10 July 1792, p.3

[43]See more details at https://simonchadwick.net/2022/03/speic-seoigheach.html

[44]*Belfast News-Letter*, Tuesday, 17 July, 1792, p.3

[45]*Belfast News-Letter*, Monday, 8 September 1794, p.3

[46]*Belfast News-Letter*, Friday, 19 June 1795, p.3

[47]*Belfast News-Letter*, Friday, 12 August 1796, p.2

[48]For this and the following quotes from minutes of the Belfast Society for Promoting Knowledge, I am indebted to John Killen, *A History of the Linen Hall Library, 1788-1988*, Belfast, 1990, pp.176-178

[49]Information from the *Bunting I* webpage of the Irish Traditional Music Association (ITMA), which quotes from Peter Downey, *Edward Bunting and the Ancient Irish Music: The Publication History of* A General Collection of the Ancient Irish Music... Adapted for the Piano-Forte *(London: Preston & Son)*, Lisburn: 2017.

[50]Cathryn Bronwyn McWilliams, *The Letters and Legacy of Mary Ann McCracken* (1770-1866), Åbo Akademi University Press, Finland, 2021, Letter 30, pp.363-365. I have added punctuation in places and filled in some missing words.

[51]The notice was reprinted the following Monday and Friday, both on page 4.

[52]Cathryn Bronwyn McWilliams, *The Letters and Legacy of Mary Ann ...* , p.402

[53]Jean Agnew and Maria Luddy, eds., *The Drennan-McTier Letters 1776–1817*, Women's History Project in association with the Irish Manuscripts Commission, Dublin, 1998–1999, vol.2, p.351.

[54]See ITMA's webpage on Bunting's 1797 *Collection*: https://www.itma.ie/features/printed-collections/edward-buntings-first-collection-of-irish-music-1797

[55]Agnew and Luddy, eds., *The Drennan-McTier Letters*, vol.2, p.373

[56] Cathryn Bronwyn McWilliams, *The Letters and Legacy of Mary Ann ...*, p.821

[57] Barra Boydell, 'The United Irishmen, Music, Harps, and National Identity', *Eighteenth-Century Ireland / Iris an dá chultúr*, vol.13, p.49

[58] Joep Leerssen, *Mere Irish and Fíor Ghael*, 2n edn., Cork, 1996, p.376

[59] Agnew and Luddy, eds., *The Drennan-McTier Letters*, vol.3, p.170

[60] Quoted in Charlotte Milligan Fox, *Annals of the Irish Harpers*, London, 1911, p.29

[61] From the first draft of O'Neill's *Memoirs*, QUB MS 4/46, 080 as dictated to Thomas Hughes.

[62] Tom Moore, *A History of the First Presbyterian Church Belfast, 1644-1983*, Belfast, 1983, p.92

[63] *Belfast News-Letter*, Friday, 3 June 1803, p.3 (also Tue 7 June, p.1 and Fri 10 June, p.4)

[64] Roy Johnston, *Bunting's 'Messiah'*, Belfast, 2003, p.61

[65] Edward Bunting, *The Ancient Music of Ireland, Arranged for the Piano Forte*, Dublin, 1840, p.73

[66] *Belfast News-Letter*, Tuesday, 14 September 1802, p.3

[67] *Belfast News-Letter*, Tuesday, 12 October 1802, p.3

[68] *Belfast News-Letter*, Tuesday, 16 July 1805, p.2; also *Belfast Commercial Chronicle*, Wednesday, 17 July 1805, p.3

[69] *Belfast News-Letter*, Friday, 5 September 1806, p.2

[70] *Belfast News-Letter*, Tuesday, 9 September 1806, p.2

[71] *Belfast Commercial Chronicle*, Saturday, 6 September 1806, p.2

[72] *Belfast News-Letter*, Tuesday, 30 August 1808, p.3

[73] Quoted in Charlotte Milligan Fox, *Annals of the Irish Harpers*, London, 1911, p.62

[74] 'P' [George Petrie], 'Our Portrait Gallery, No.XLI', *Dublin University Magazine*, vol.29, no.169, January 1847.

[75] Ibid.

[76] *Belfast News-Letter*, Tuesday, 14 June 1808, p.2, *Belfast Commercial Chronicle*, Wednesday, 15 June 1808, p.2, and *Freeman's Journal*, Thursday, 16 June 1808, p.4

[77] David Byers, 'Bunting's Airs, Graces and Harps', *Perspectives*, Cruit Éireann / Harp Ireland, April 2022, p.12

[78] Ian Woodfield, 'Songs my mother taught me: new light on James Macpherson's Ossian', *Journal of the Society for Musicology in Ireland*, 2021, vol. 16, p.3, accessed 30 May 2022. DOI: https://doi.org/10.35561/JSMI16211

[79] *Belfast News-Letter*, Tuesday, 23 August 1808, p.3

[80] Quoted in Charlotte Milligan Fox, *Annals of the Irish Harpers*, London, 1911, pp.221-222

[81] Ibid. pp.222-223

[82] *Belfast News-Letter*, Friday, 4 November 1808, p.2

[83] *Belfast Commercial Chronicle*, Monday, 20 March 1809, p.2

[84] A Subscriber, 'The Ancient Music of Ireland adapted to the Piano Forte', *The Belfast Monthly Magazine*, vol. 2, No. 8 (Mar. 31, 1809), pp. 191-193

[85] *Belfast Commercial Chronicle*, Saturday, 21 October 1809, p.4

[86] *Belfast Monthly Magazine*, vol.3, no.14, 30 September 1809, p.183

[87] Quoted in Charlotte Milligan Fox, *Annals of the Irish Harpers*, London, 1911, p.225-226

[88] Cathryn Bronwyn McWilliams, *The Letters and Legacy of Mary Ann ...* Letter 146, pp.667, 668. Sent to Robert James Tennent, dated 27 September 1849

[89] *Belfast News-Letter*, Tuesday, 28 March 1809, p.3

[90] *Belfast News-Letter*, Friday 22 December 1809, p.2. The *Belfast Commercial Chronicle* published its report on Saturday 23 December 1809, p.2 and that was reprinted in *The Irish Magazine or Monthly Asylum for Neglected Biography*, January 1810, pp.5-7

[91] *Belfast News-Letter*, Friday, 4 January 1811, p.3

[92] *Belfast Commercial Chronicle*, Saturday, 25 May 1811, p.2

[93] *Belfast Commercial Chronicle*, Wednesday, 25 November 1812, p.4

[94] *Belfast News-Letter*, Tuesday, 22 June 1813, p.2

[95] *Dublin Evening Post*, Tuesday, 30 January 1816, p.2

[96] Aiken McClelland, 'The Irish Harp Society' in *Ulster Folklife*, vol 21, 1975, p.18

[97] *Belfast News-Letter*, Friday, 1 March 1816, p.2

[98] *Belfast News-Letter*, Tuesday, 5 November 1816, p.3

[99] John Gamble, *A View of society and manners in the North of Ireland in the summer and autumn of 1812, etc.*, London, 1813, p.66

[100]'P' [George Petrie], 'Our Portrait Gallery, No.XLI', *Dublin University Magazine*, vol.29, no.169, January 1847.

[101]See the pdf *Stephen White organ-builder* at https://www.byersmusic.com/edward-bunting.php#Bunting06

[102]Uncredited quotations here and hereafter are from the printed minutes and resolutions of the Irish Harp Society, dated 16 April 1819, from the Beath collection in the Linen Hall Library.

[103]Aiken McClelland, 'The Irish Harp Society' in *Ulster Folklife*, vol 21, 1975, p.19

[104]*Belfast News-Letter*, Tuesday, 4 May 1819, p.2; *Dublin Evening Post*, Thursday, 6 May 1819, p.4; the *Military Register* (quoting the *Belfast Commercial Chronicle*), Wednesday, 19 May 1819, p.18

[105]*Bombay Gazette*, Wednesday, 15 September 1819, p.3

[106]*Belfast News-Letter*, Friday, 1 October 1819, p.3

[107]*Report of the Irish Harp Society* (Belfast, 1821), Bunting Collection, Queen's University, Belfast, quoted in Aiken McClelland, 'The Irish Harp Society' in *Ulster Folklife*, vol.21, 1975, p.19

[108]Micheál McDermott, 'Patrick Byrne of Magheracloone, leading Harper and distinguished celebrity of the Nineteenth Century.' *Clogher Record*, vol. 20, no. 2, Clogher Historical Society, 2010, p.225 and p.227

[109]Joseph Gardiner, Ulster Journal of Archaeology, Second Series, 1, 1895, p.151, quoted in Aiken McClelland, 'The Irish Harp Society', p.24

[110]Robert Bruce Armstrong, *Musical Instruments, Part 1, The Irish and the Highland Harps*, Edinburgh, 1904, p.52

[111]*Belfast Commercial Chronicle*, Monday 7 January 1822, p.3

[112]*Belfast News-Letter*, Tuesday 26 September 1837, p.2

[113]Linen Hall Library, Beath Collection, IR/BEA/Box 6 (16)

[114]Edward Bunting, *The Ancient Music of Ireland, Arranged for the Piano Forte*, Dublin, 1840, p.66

[115]Quoted in Charlotte Milligan Fox, *Annals of the Irish Harpers*, London, 1911, pp.274-275

[116]Grainne Yeats, *The Harp of Ireland*, Belfast, 1992, p.30

[117]Quoted in Charlotte Milligan Fox, *Annals*, p.304-305 and in Cathryn Bronwyn McWilliams, *The Letters and Legacy ...* Letter 127, p.594

**Cruit Éireann | Harp Ireland** was established in 2016 by harpers in collaboration with The Arts Council, An Chomhairle Ealaíon to support the continuing evolution of the harp in Ireland. Our vision for the harp is that it will attract more performers, inspire new audiences and enrich musical and cultural life on the island of Ireland.

*For more information visit harpireland.ie*

## ACKNOWLEDGEMENTS

Thanks to David Byers for helping us mark the 230th anniversary of the celebrated 1792 meeting of harpers in Belfast with a truly authoritative text. We are grateful to each of our funders for their financial support and to The Irish Pages Press/ Cló An Mhíl Bhuí for its dedication and professionalism.